ROUTLEDGE LIBRARY EDITIONS:
TRANSPORT ECONOMICS

Volume 17

THE PRINCIPAL FACTORS IN FREIGHT TRAIN OPERATING

THE PRINCIPAL FACTORS IN FREIGHT TRAIN OPERATING

PHILIP BURTT

Routledge
Taylor & Francis Group
LONDON AND NEW YORK

First published in 1923 by George Allen & Unwin Ltd.
Revised edition 1924

This edition first published in 2017
by Routledge
2 Park Square, Milton Park, Abingdon, Oxon OX14 4RN

and by Routledge
711 Third Avenue, New York, NY 10017

Routledge is an imprint of the Taylor & Francis Group, an informa business

British Library Cataloguing in Publication Data
A catalogue record for this book is available from the British Library

ISBN: 978-0-415-78484-9 (Set)
ISBN: 978-1-315-20175-7 (Set) (ebk)
ISBN: 978-1-138-63263-9 (Volume 17) (hbk)
ISBN: 978-1-315-20809-1 (Volume 17) (ebk)

Publisher's Note
The publisher has gone to great lengths to ensure the quality of this reprint but points out that some imperfections in the original copies may be apparent.

Disclaimer
The publisher has made every effort to trace copyright holders and would welcome correspondence from those they have been unable to trace.

THE PRINCIPAL FACTORS IN FREIGHT TRAIN OPERATING

BY

PHILIP BURTT

LONDON: GEORGE ALLEN & UNWIN LTD.
RUSKIN HOUSE, 40 MUSEUM STREET, W.C. 1

First published . . . . July 1923
Second Edition (Revised) January 1924

Printed in Great Britain by
UNWIN BROTHERS, LIMITED, THE GRESHAM PRESS, LONDON AND WOKING

PREFACE

THE contents of the following pages embody an attempt to put into book form the lectures which I have delivered from copious notes at the London School of Economics under the heading which I have adopted as the title of this book. I have had for the purposes of publication not only to extend the notes, but also to enlarge the scope of the ground they cover, and to make more definite the concrete illustrations of the methods and instructions of the railway companies which I have been permitted to make use of.

I am indebted to two of our General Managers, Mr. Arthur Watson, of the London and North-Western Railway, and Mr. R. L. Wedgwood, of the North-Eastern Railway—now General Managers of the London, Midland and Scottish and the London and North Eastern Companies respectively—for permission to use a number of tables and figures extracted from their working regulations and instructions to staff; and I desire also to record my thanks to Mr. Watson's assistant, Mr. W. E. Preston, for the amount of time and care which he has given to going through my MS. and making a number of valuable suggestions.

I have necessarily had to adhere to the names of the various railway companies as we have known them up to the end of last year, for the book has been compiled during the past two years; but the reader will remember that where the name of a railway company is mentioned it has now become a section of a larger whole. It will doubtless be a good many years before all the old landmarks are removed; and for statistical comparison with the past it will be almost essential to retain the old areas of train working for a considerable period.

Two reasons have weighed with me in yielding to many requests to publish these lectures. Firstly, the great dearth which exists in Great Britain of literary matter in the form of textbooks dealing specifically with railway operating problems—at a time when railway students are more numerous probably than at any previous period and more eager than ever to tackle the problems dealt with; and secondly, because I believe that the more that expert intelligence can be directed to these problems of freight train operation the more clearly and speedily will it be realised what a vast scope exists for the further development of the processes of reform and improvement in method which are constantly referred to in these pages as having been begun, and which the new revelations of science on its applied side have placed within the reach of railway officers.

From these considerations I am particularly grateful to the railway managers for the help they have given me in preparing the volume.

The book is essentially one for students. It does not claim to have any merit as a work of literature; indeed, in this direction I am only too conscious of its defects.

PHILIP BURTT.

15, St. John's Wood Park, N.W. 8.
March 31, 1923.

CONTENTS

ILLUSTRATIONS

INTRODUCTORY

THE IMPORTANCE OF THE TRAIN LOAD PROBLEM

It is a trite saying in these days that in all branches of industry a new outlook is necessary if there is to be any considerable development of new enterprise in the commercial world. But in the railway world it is more than a trite saying. A new era comes into being as the Railways Act of 1921 takes effect and the internal re-organisation which the Act requires is coupled with a new incentive.

It places public service on behalf of the community as the *raison d'être* of a railway company's existence rather than the private gain of shareholders, and many of the advantages it secures to the railways are contingent upon such *motif* being duly recognised and given effect to.

The problem now before the small but powerful group of controllers of the great railway system of this country is a difficult one, especially when it is remembered that owing to high wages and high costs all round it is only by Government subsidies (now discontinued) that financial solvency has during recent years been maintained, and if it were not for the conviction that there is great possibility of economies in working costs under the new *régime*, the problem might be written down as insoluble.

It is well to remember that the railway organisation is in reality a machine—the largest machine in the country, having for its main object the creation of wealth and the extension of its capital resources—and, partly because of its vastness, *it is capable of almost limitless improvement and development*. Like the locomotive, which is its main tool, it is constantly growing larger and more effective.

One—and perhaps the most important—aspect of the

railway problem will be how to render the great machine, the railway system itself, capable of carrying with minimum increase in capital expenditure an ever increasing volume of railway traffic. The traffic carrying capacity of the railway system will have to be enlarged, and there are four directions in which such increased capacity can be secured, namely :—

(1) A general extension and enlargement of running lines, sidings, and terminal accommodation, involving the expenditure of additional capital. This is perhaps the easiest, as it is the most expensive, method of procedure: a continuous expenditure of new capital in the future will probably be essential to satisfactory working of an increased volume of traffic, but it is not so effective a method of dealing with the needs of the future as any of the three following alternatives; and it will be found that the need for fresh capital expenditure will be reduced just as progressive development under the headings (2), (3), and (4) takes place.

(2) A steady improvement in working in the way of increased freight train loads and wagon loads: this development has made considerable headway within the last twenty years—in other countries in much greater degree than our own. The records of these last twenty years alone are sufficient to show the great scope there is for further increased improvement along the same line; but the facts of unification of working under a federation of railway management, and of a *régime* of co-operation instead of competition between railway systems, will also inevitably increase, and increase greatly, this scope and opportunity.

(3) An improvement in the speed or rate of movement of locomotives, trains, and traffic by improvement of the railway organisation on its mechanical side, such as by improved signalling, more efficient brakes, or in the description of power used, e.g. electricity as tractive power in place of steam. The possibility of increased speed is immense, not only as regards the actual speed of train movement, which would be the

necessary sequel to such a change as, for instance, the adoption of continuous brakes on goods wagons, or of more rapid acceleration in starting which is one of the main advantages secured by electric traction; but by the elimination of delays in shunting, by the reduction of engine time at terminal stations, and time getting to and from the shed, etc. For all this engine time outside of that occupied in the actual train work is included in the statistical unit of "engine hours" as distinct from "train engine hours."[1]

(4) More vigorous human energy in all directions. This is a powerful factor, and affords great hope. More education on the part of the staff generally, or greater intelligence and wider outlook on the managerial side, more vigour and keenness throughout the rank and file to assist the management in improving the load and increasing everywhere the rate of movement; and (perhaps above all) a general and all-round development of a spirit of co-operation and goodwill, as fellow-workers in a common service for the benefit of the commonwealth. All these factors count for much.

But this little treatise is intended to deal specially with all the circumstances and factors which have a bearing upon heading (2) of the directions above indicated in which improvement may be expected—the question of loads of trains and wagons. It is a many-sided question, and involves much technical detail and much close observation. The treatment of the question in the following chapters is intended to form a textbook for the large number of railwaymen who are engaged in one way or another in the manipulation of railway traffic for conveyance, to all of whom the train load factor must be one of daily interest.

[1] The standard statistics (as now issued monthly by the Ministry of Transport) deal with the two units of "Engine Hours" and "Train Engine Hours." The former include all the hours an engine is at work, such as time occupied in getting to and from the engine shed, time occupied in shunting, time at terminal points away from home; the train engine hours are only the hours when the engine is earning revenue with its train. So that acceleration of speed in train working improves the train hours of effective work; reduction of time occupied in shunting, or in getting to and from work, etc., reduces the engine hours unit and increases the miles worked per engine hour.

The other three features will be referred to from time to time, but as subsidiary to the question of improvement of load, which is the underlying theme throughout the book.

The attitude of the rank and file of railwaymen is an important factor, and the speeding up or improvement of the machine as a whole is perhaps more dependent on the men working whole-heartedly to make the railway system an efficient public service than upon any other single factor. Any slowing down or "ca' canny" policy is probably but a temporary phase.

The main part of this book has been compiled during the two past years in connection with lectures at the London School of Economics, but the insertion of various notes in places and careful revision will have prevented it from becoming in any respect out of date. Events in the world of transport move rapidly in these days. The new Railways Act, 1921, is an accomplished fact; and the large number of railway systems in Great Britain outside of the metropolitan area are already reduced to four large group companies, within the frontiers of each of which the scope is now vastly increased both for the application of working economies such as are pointed out herein, and for the more rapid extension of the improved methods which have been already adopted in more prescribed areas.

At the outset, Chapter I begins with an attempt to answer the simple but pertinent question, What is a train load? When we are told of an engine hauling a load of 15,000 tons of coal in America, we know that by the load is meant the gross train load behind the locomotive—the total weight of wagons and contents which the engine can haul. But when we learn that the average train load of coal from a given district to an adjacent port is 600 tons, or that the average train load over the whole of the American railways is 650 tons, we must realise that this figure only refers to the freight contents of the train which the wagons carry and on which the conveyance charges are levied. The expression "train load" is commonly used, therefore, with different meanings by railwaymen, and the student must therefore be careful in his terminology. This is a preliminary caution as to two entirely different meanings that the word loosely used may convey, apart altogether from the quantitative analysis of a train load which the expert has to undertake, and which distinguishes him from the unskilled student. A train load may, it will be seen, vary from a few tons up to about 15,000. It should now be appreciated that more is involved in the query, "What is a train load?" than at first appears, and the first two chapters of this book are taken up in trying to adequately answer the question.

The problem of how to measure and how to improve the train load on our British railways is one of the foremost at the root of the great question of how to secure greater economy in the operation of train working, and no apology is needed for labouring the point, for it is as the keystone in the arch of efficiency in the equipment of the British railway officer who is to be successful in conducting transportation.

When we read that the average train load of goods traffic in America is 950 tons on the Pennsylvania R.R., and not less than 650 tons over the whole of the railways in the U.S.A., whilst on the railways at home it does not exceed 135 tons, the figures are so striking that we can no longer dismiss the matter with the remark "conditions are different!" The nature of the differences must be considered and measured.

The movement for an improved and enlarged train load for goods traffic was started in earnest on the North Eastern Railway in England in 1901 and 1902, and fortunately we have some records which the General Manager of that company has published which show us something of the possibilities of economy which result from train load improvement. These figures, when placed alongside of the tonnage of traffic conveyed and the number of engines employed by the N.E.R., show that, whilst there was a continuous growth in traffic (up to the date of the war), the number of miles run by trains steadily diminished after 1902, and the number of engines employed by the company, which went up almost by leaps and bounds during the last twenty years of the last century, was actually reduced in 1904 by relegating 142 to "the scrap-heap," and the reduced number then employed has been sufficient to deal with the traffic ever since—at least until 1918. I deal with these figures in fuller detail in the last chapter of this book: and here I only insert the figures showing the improved goods train loads and the reducing train mileage up to the year before the war.

NORTH EASTERN RAILWAY.

Year.	Average Freight Train Load, Tons.	Freight Train Mileage.	Year.	Average Freight Train Load, Tons.	Freight Train Mileage.
1902	81·4	14,932,815	1908	115·6	11,861,217
1903	92·4	13,379,129	1909	122·9	11,376 578
1904	100·2	12,215,620	1910	126·5	11,326,338
1905	106·7	11,729,849	1911	127·8	11,386,545
1906	109·9	12,338,303	1912	131·1	11,074 [illegible]28
1907	114·7	12,937,650	1913	131·7	12,312,151

Generally speaking, the British railway worker is only just beginning to apply the tonnage unit in calculating the loads of the trains he is dealing with. It has in the past been considered sufficient to measure the train load in wagons, but the day for this method is going by. A load cannot be accurately measured in wagons, for a wagon is now almost as variable a factor as a train. It may be anything from 5 tons to 50 tons in weight, just as a British train load of freight may be anything from 15 tons to 1,500. If the " new era " is to usher in anything like scientific accuracy in train working, loads of trains must be measured in tons, length of journey must be measured in miles, speeds must be carefully measured in miles per hour; and the effective work of transportation must be measured or regarded as so many ton miles operated in a given unit of time—the engine hour.

To be accurate in the application of figures may make the task of the trainmen a little more difficult, though the arithmetic required is, as a rule, not much more than simple addition. It will, however, make the work of better quality, and tend to make the railway servant engaged in it of higher rank also; and he will enjoy his work the more.

The movement for calculating freight train loads in

tons was making good headway in 1914 when war broke out; and one inevitable but unfortunate result of the war was to stop for the time being this amongst many other movements for increased efficiency in railway working, when all available human energy and intellect had to be drafted from the peaceful channels of industry to the demands and economically destructive purposes of war.

The Principal Factors in Freight Train Operating

CHAPTER I

THE NET FREIGHT TRAIN LOAD

THIS chapter deals with the freight train load. How many of my readers, I wonder, have any clear idea of what is the load stated in tons of an average or typical goods train in Great Britain ? The " train load " may be given either as the aggregate figure of weight of the wagons plus the freight contents, the total weight which the locomotive is hauling, i.e. the gross load ; or the " train load " may refer to the freight contents only ; it is then known as the " net freight load "—the subject of this chapter.

Let us look at the figures of an ordinary typical mixed freight train. I say typical rather than average, for the one I set out in the table on page 20 is a sample of what would usually be regarded as a well loaded train. It is taken more or less at randon—the record of an actual train running from station " A " to station " B " on August 2, 1918. The weights and description of each wagon and its contents are set out in detail, and we shall refer to it from time to time.

We shall notice that the load consisted of 61 wagons, having a tare weight of 368 tons 1 cwt. ; and a contents weight or net freight load of 350 tons 14 cwt., giving a gross train load of 718 tons 15 cwt. From this it will also be seen that the average tare weight of each wagon was 6 tons 0¾ cwt., and that each wagon carried an average

PARTICULARS OF TRAFFIC ON 7.40 P.M. GOODS TRAIN FROM STATION "A" TO STATION "B," AUGUST 2, 1918.

Wagon No. and Owner.		Open or Covered.	Wagon Tare.	Weight of Contents.	Nature of Contents.
			T. C.	T. C.	
N.E. ..	101167	O.	8 3	1 17 E *	Pit props
Mid. ..	19111	O.	4 16	3 4 E	Pit props
G.W. ..	75264	O.	5 10	4 10 E	Timber
G.W. ..	21526	O.	5 19	4 1 E	Timber
L. & N.W.	11809	O.	6 0	4 0 E	Timber
G.E. ..	23183	O.	5 5	4 15 E	Pit props
N.E. ..	7455	C.	6 3	1 17 E	General
N.E. ..	J. 156	O.	6 6	3 15 E	Iron pipes
G.N. ..	63251	O.	5 4	4 16 E	Cement
L.B.S.C. ..	2025	O.	5 19	7 6	Flour
N.E. (H.B.)	386	C.	9 0	2 10	Cake
N.E. (H.B.)	388	C.	8 19	2 10	Cake
G.N. ..	27830	O.	5 6	6 0	Flour
G.N.S. ..	1649	O.	5 4	6 0	Flour
G.E. ..	32150	O.	5 7	4 1	General
N.E. ..	76	O.	5 6	7 7	Tin
L. & N.W.	23934	O.	5 18	4 0	Flour
Mid. ..	99868	O.	5 0	5 4	Flour
L. & Y. ..	14457	O.	4 17	4 11	Flour
N.E. ..	98541	C.	6 10	10 0	Flour
N.E. ..	78046	O.	7 1	7 15	Flour
L. & Y. ..	897	O.	4 11	5 17	Flour
Mid. ..	111388	O.	4 18	5 3	Flour
L. & N.W.	50710	O.	6 17	7 0	Cake
G.W. ..	64632	O.	5 8	4 0	Flour
G.W. ..	4492	O.	5 17	6 18	Flour
C.L.C. ..	351	O.	5 10	4 10	Oats
G.W. ..	15634	O.	6 8	1 12 E	General
N.E. ..	78507	C.	9 12	1 8 E	General
Mid. ..	12587	O.	4 18	3 2 E	Castings
N.E. ..	90641	C.	8 0	2 0 E	Block lead
G.C. ..	14711	O.	5 6	2 14 E	Oil
Mid. ..	112552	O.	6 15	11 5 E	Iron Ore
N.B. ..	56460	O.	5 14	7 6 E	Iron ore
Mid. ..	105187	O.	5 9	2 11 E	Laths
N.E. ..	61647	C.	6 14	8 7	Flour
N.E. ..	74306	C.	6 3	1 17	General
L. & Y. ..	11176	C.	6 2	1 17 E	General
N.E. ..	98542	C.	6 13	3 7 E	General
L. & Y. ..	9368	C.	6 9	1 11 E	General
C.L.C. ..	2893	C.	6 10	3 10 E	General
N.E. ..	37896	C.	7 1	2 19 E	General
N.B. ..	49113	C.	6 14	3 5 E	Tranships, etc.
L. & Y. ..	20476	C.	3 16	3 0	Horse food
N.E. ..	100818	C.	6 10	3 10 E	General
G.C. ..	32325	O.	5 18	9 6	Flour
N.E. ..	81361	O.	6 5	10 0	Gravel
N.E. ..	74437	O.	6 4	10 0	Gravel
N.E. ..	37574	O.	6 5	10 0	Gravel
N.E. ..	83553	O.	6 1	10 0	Gravel
N.S. ..	1947	O.	6 10	10 0 E	Copper ore
N.S. ..	4552	O.	4 19	8 0 E	Copper ore
N.S. ..	3209	O.	5 0	10 0 E	Copper ore
G.N.S. ..	1939	O.	5 7	8 0 E	Copper ore
L. & S.W.	7942	O.	5 10	8 0 E	Copper ore
N.E. ..	23854	O.	6 4	12 0 E	Copper ore
Fur. ..	4750	O.	5 17	10 0 E	Copper ore
Fur. ..	1944	O.	5 12	10 0 E	Copper ore
Mid. ..	52901	O.	5 1	8 0 E	Copper ore
L. & Y. ..	15321	O.	5 10	9 10 E	Copper ore
L. & Y. ..	17778	O.	5 10	9 10 E	Copper ore
Total Number of Wagons		61	368 1	350 14	

Total Gross Weight .. .. 718 tons 15 cwt.

* E = Estimated weight.

freight load of 5 tons 15 cwt. The average *loaded* wagon (weight and contents) was 11 tons 15¾ cwt.

So much for the record of this specific train ; but even though I have ventured to call this load a good one, the reader has not as yet before him the evidence to enable him to form his own view as to the goodness or poorness of such a load in comparison with any general average.

Let me then set out further concrete illustrations of goods trains, for it will be well at the outset to thoroughly acquaint ourselves with the facts. Some years ago, when the "Tubes" were under construction in London, a large contract for the supply of iron segments for the tube lining was secured by a firm of ironfounders at Stockton-on-Tees, and in order that the traffic might be forwarded by railway a very low rate was quoted in competition with water carriage. A stipulation was made that the traffic should be conveyed regularly in train loads of 45 wagons and 8 tons per wagon, or 360 tons of iron per train, despatched every other day, or three days per week. We have here a freight load of 360 tons, and as each wagon weighed about 5½ tons and the van was 15 tons in weight, the gross load represented 622½ tons.

A second case I would quote is that of special loads of grain which were some years ago worked (again in competition with water) from seaport to inland mill in loads of 600 tons of freight. In this case each train consisted of 50 wagons, each wagon having a tare weight of 6 tons and a capacity of 12 tons, the grain being carried loose in bulk. So the gross load of each train was 900 tons (920 including brake van), and with such a good revenue earning load the importing miller secured a very advantageously low rate. It will be seen that in this case not only was the load a large one, but the relation between revenue earning or net freight load and the gross load was very satisfactory. The revenue load was about 65 per cent. of the gross. (In the train of iron segments the percentage ratio was only 59 per cent. ; in the typical mixed train set out on page 20 the ratio was only 49 per cent.)

Bearing in mind this ratio of freight load to gross load (65 per cent.), we may regard it as a high percentage, and it would not be easy to find many cases of goods trains in England so satisfactory as this. They were, however, only of a temporary nature, and I have no records to surpass them except in the case of coal conveyed in high capacity wagons.

We may now speak of *the average goods train load* in Great Britain: we are better equipped for estimating the meaning of an average now that we have made ourselves conversant with a few concrete cases of actual train loads.

We may, I think, put to one side the comment often made that as it is the business of a railwayman to deal with practical concrete realities, the average unit is of little value. Averages are important as historical records: they are essential for the purposes of comparison; and much of the effective thinking in regard to great practical problems must of necessity be done by the use of averages. Then again, it is important that the practical railwayman should, at least occasionally, *take time* to think: the successful manager must constantly do so. The writer remembers a leading general manager who caused much amusement to a subordinate officer who asked his chief where he was going to spend the Whitsuntide week-end holiday, and received the prompt reply: "I am going home *to think!*"

Averages, then, are essential for accurate thinking in railway management. Look at the following table of average train loads, taken from Mossop's *Railway Operating Statistics*, with certain additions which I have made for comparison purposes.

The figures given (see next page), which are the record of N.E.R. results, are probably typical of what has been going on in England as a whole during the years in question.

There is a slight tendency towards improvement shown in Mossop's figures, but on the whole the results, and the fact that 65 per cent. of the load is dead weight hauled and only 35 per cent. is earning revenue, seems disappointing, if this may be taken as typical of English freight train working. The fact comes out in bolder relief when this average result is taken in conjunction with the grain train illustration of 600 tons of revenue load out of 920 gross. This was equal to 65 per cent., and it may be said to represent the high-water mark of revenue earning loads so far as a goods train is concerned.

Let us see what we man gather by a careful study of the table set out below. It is a record of progress in more than one direction. From the traffic operating point of view, special attention should be given to the facts revealed in columns 2, 3, and 4.

The net freight (average) load on the whole system went up from 92·4 to 126·5 tons, a large increase in seven years—about 36 per cent. The gross weight of the trains

NORTH EASTERN RAILWAY ENGINES.

Average Train Loads and Engine Hauling Capacities.

Year. 1.	Gross Train Load. 2.	Freight Load. 3.	Freight Loads Percentage of Gross Load. 4.	Average Capacity N.E.R. Freight Engines. 5.	Gross Loads Percentage of Average Capacity. 6.
1903	275·5	92·4	33·54	603	45·7
1904	294·4	100·2	34·04	612	48·1
1905	310·4	106·7	34·38	628	49·4
1906	318·0	109·9	34·56	635	50·0
1907	326·9	114·7	35·09	642	51·0
1908	333·6	115·6	34·65	661	50·4
1909	351·8	122·9	34·93	666	52·8
1910	362·8	126·5	34·87	671	54·1

Capacity of *heaviest* freight engine, Class "T":—At 20 m.p.h., 1,215 tons; at 15 m.p.h., 1,350 tons.

increased at the same time from 275·5 to 362·8—about 32 per cent. The ratio between freight and gross load, as column 4 indicates, showed much fluctuation. It improved during the first four years, whilst during the last four years of the period it retrograded; on the eight-year period, however, there was on the whole a slight improvement in the relation between the freight or revenue load and the gross weight of trains.

But the important figure for us here is the actual average weight of freight load, whilst it seems little enough as we bear in mind the three concrete cases already set out on pages 20 and 21. The improvement in these years is good, and we must try to realise the effect of the large increase in the eight years : fewer trains all round, giving greater line capacity throughout the system ; a smaller number of engines employed ; economy in rolling stock ; and probably the obviation of additional capital expenditure on a large scale. But these general considerations will be again referred to at a later stage ; the table is exhibited here to draw attention to the figure of average freight load of 126·5 tons and the progress made during the years set out.

We shall consider more encouraging figures when we come to deal with coal trains, or ironstone trains. The freight will often represent some 60 to 70 per cent. of the gross load. The load of mineral trains, however, is generally in one direction only, and the empty wagon haulage on the return trip is an important factor which has to be set off against the economical loading of the trains on the outward journey. Of the loads of mineral trains, however, we shall have much to say in later chapters.

As a summary of the principal facts and figures so far given we may quote comparative figures for 1910 given by Mr. Mossop [1] of gross and freight loads, to which I have added average and maximum engine capacity.

Year 1910—N.E.R.

Average freight load	126.9	tons
Average gross load	362·8	,,
Average engine capacity	671	,,
Maximum engine capacity—		
At 20 m.p.h.	1,215	,,
At 15 m.p.h.	1,350	,,

This reference to the statistics of the N.E.R. may be considered as past history ; but, especially when taken in conjunction with other statistical results set out in the chapter on statistics, they may be regarded as lessons from the past which have a very direct bearing upon the possibilities of the immediate future. A great authority has said that the prime use of statistics of past records is that when intelligently and accurately presented they throw clear light upon the trend of events in the future.

[1] *Railway Operating Statistics*, p. 41.

But let us bring our statistics for freight train loads more up to date. We have now the opportunity of studying each company's average freight train load, and the monthly variations, from the statistics published by the Ministry of Transport. The following table gives the average freight load, taken from the official returns, for each of the principal railway companies in Great Britain for the two years 1920 and 1921 :—

Railway Company.	Average Freight Train Load in Tons.	
	1921.	1920.
Great Central	153·3	169·7
Great Eastern	105·9	112·7
Great Northern	144·5	159·2
Great Western	133·6	146·5
Lancashire and Yorkshire	117·5	129·0
London and North-Western	127·6	142·5
London and South-Western	103·6	105·3
Midland	128·3	144·0
North-Eastern	140·11	153·6
Total freight trains in Great Britain ..	121·2	132·5

I do not propose at this moment to attempt to draw any lessons or any conclusions from the figures here presented. They should be studied carefully by every student of railway statistics, as they will be followed carefully by every responsible traffic officer. I would merely remark that the more the facts behind these figures are studied and examined, the clearer comes out the great scope there is for further improvement of the train load. It must be remembered that we have had since 1914 many years of war disturbance which seriously interfered with improvements in train working. But such evidence as we have of progressive improvement in loads in England since the beginning of the century may be considered as satisfactory so far as it goes. It will be noticed that the North Eastern Railway's average freight train load, given on page 23 at 126·5 tons in 1910, had increased to 153·6 in 1920. (1921 was an exceptional year on account of an abnormal reduction in coal traffic.) The point of more immediate importance is the scope which undoubtedly exists for further progress in the same direction.

At a later stage we shall give careful attention to the various methods by which improved loading of goods trains can be further encouraged and secured. For the moment we would merely summarise them as follows :—

1. By an increase in the number of loaded wagons per train, either (*a*) by the use of more powerful engines, or (*b*) by a reduction of empty wagon haulage.
2. By the provision of larger capacity wagons, and a reduction of the tare ratio to carrying capacity of each wagon.
3. By the increased loading of each wagon.
4. By improved transhipping arrangements.
5. By the encouragement of the despatch of wagon and train load consignments by the quotation of favourable rates to traders for large quantities.

The possibility of improvement under every one of these heads has been greatly enhanced lately by the new grouping of railway companies; in introducing the Ministry of Transport Bill in 1919 the Minister designate as he then was stated that the time had come when a new spirit of co-operation between the railway companies must supersede the exaggerated form of competition which had hitherto marked the railway *régime*, and that some more unified control must be established, if the railway systems of Great Britain are to be economically and efficiently governed.

Following this preliminary survey of figures of freight train loads in Great Britain, we may with advantage consider what has been going on in America. It may be of academic interest only, but whether academic or practical, the records from that land whose delight seems to be in big things are extraordinary enough.

In the published statistics of American railroads all these figures are set out with much completeness. If we take three of the big trunk railroads east of Chicago, e.g. the Pennsylvania, the New York Central and the

Baltimore and Ohio railroads, we find the figures are as follows :—

YEAR 1920.

	Average Train Load.
	Revenue Tonnage.
Pennsylvania Railroad	948·73
New York Central Railroad	835·07
Baltimore and Ohio Railroad ..	868·88

The Interstate Commerce Commission Annual Reports have published the average loads of all railways since 1888, and as the record presents so telling a story of progress I set out the figures in detail as follows :—

AVERAGE FREIGHT TRAIN LOAD ON THE AMERICAN RAILWAYS SINCE 1888.

Year.	Average Train Load in Tons.	Year.	Average Train Load in Tons.	Year.	Average Train Load in Tons.
1888	176	1899	243	1910	380
1889	179	1900	270	1911	383
1890	175	1901	281	1912	430
1891	181	1902	296	1913	445
1892	181	1903	310	1914	452
1893	183	1904	307	1915	474
1894	179	1905	322	1916	488
1895	189	1906	344	1917	521
1896	198	1907	357	1918	546
1897	204	1908	352	1919	556
1898	226	1909	363	1920	647

It may be noted that whilst the present-day figures in America are four or five times as large as our British averages, thirty-four years ago the average American load was no greater than that obtaining on some of our railway systems at home to-day ; but the figure has gone steadily up ever since our railway confrères across the Atlantic began to apply to railway working more scientific methods and records.

I would only add about these figures that they are not presented to my readers with any expectation that English railways will follow till they reach the American standard. British methods must fit British conditions, and America must adapt her own arrangements to her own requirements.

I have stated that whilst the "gross train load" is a statistical unit of value to the operating and engineering officers, the "freight load" is of especial interest to the traffic or goods manager and the officers on the commercial side.

I have also referred to the quotation of lower rates for large quantities forwarded at one time as one method of securing more economical loads, and I propose therefore before closing this chapter to say a few words upon this particular aspect of the matter—train load rates. The other of the five methods for securing improved loading of goods trains will be fully dealt with in subsequent chapters.

Train load rates have been quoted at various times and have led to the development of new traffic or have secured traffic to a railway route which would otherwise have been conveyed by water. A very interesting case of development of traffic leading to consolidation of a railway company's position is related by Mr. E. A. Pratt [1] of one of the early railways of Holland. The Holland Iron Railway Company was first constructed between Rotterdam, Haarlem and Amsterdam, and was afterwards extended to the German frontier as the Dutch-Rhenish Railway. For a long time it could get no traffic to yield any substantial revenue in competition with the Dutch waterways, and it appeared to be a white elephant. It was only after two enterprising British gentlemen went over to Holland—one to supervise the working of the two coalmines in Westphalia, the other to act as goods manager to the railway—came to some agreement as to working mineral traffic by the new railway that the success of the latter was secured.

The result of inquiries as to working costs showed that a rate of 1 cent. per ton per kilometre (one-fifth of a penny a ton mile) would cover all transportation costs, if only the coal traffic was handed to the railway, so that it could be conveyed in lots of 200 tons at a time and in 20 wagons of 10 tons

[1] *Railways and their Rates*, p. 272, *et seq.*

each. In the converse direction, i.e. Rotterdam to Westphalia, the coal wagons were to be filled up with Spanish iron ore, a cheap rate of one shilling and threepence a ton being quoted for this back loading of the ore for 150 miles. The service of loading and unloading was to be performed by the trader, and the agreement stipulated for a quantity of not less than 62,000 tons in one year.

The arrangement was made and the opportunity for the flow of traffic existed, but for many years the result was small. When, however, Mr. W. C. Robinson went to Amsterdam in 1859 (he was British Consul at Amsterdam for many years) the arrangement began to take effect; and ultimately, mainly owing to this train load low rate on coal from Westphalia, traffic began to rapidly develop and the success of the railway became assured.

The shares of the company, which at one time had been worthless on the market, ran up to 159 per cent. on par value. In 1904, 2,000,000 tons of coal were being conveyed instead of the stipulated 62,000. The Dutch-Rhenish Railway was the forerunner of the present state-assisted Holland Railway, which operates at the present time 600 miles of railway in Holland.

I have already earlier in this chapter referred to two cases of train loads of traffic for which exceptionally low train load rates were quoted: let me now enlarge a little upon the circumstances of each. The first case I mentioned was that of the conveyance of tube "segments" from Stockton to London when the London Tubes were under construction, and the railway companies concerned gave a reduced rate of 10s. a ton (the normal "special" rate for a train load being 15s. a ton) on condition that loads of 8 tons per truck and not less than 40 wagons at one time were handed to the company, the special lot of traffic consisting of 110,000 tons; and to be conveyed in the three and a quarter years between September 1902 and December 31, 1905. In this case the railway company was relieved of all terminal service, the loading and unloading being done in the traders' sidings; and the receipts were equivalent to 13s. 4d. per train mile, or 4d. a wagon mile, leaving the cost of return working of empty wagons out of the calculation.

As a matter of fact the sea competition had not a little to do with this transaction, and had not this very low rate by rail been quoted, the traffic would undoubtedly have been carried to London by water. But this traffic was, there can be no doubt, a valuable traffic for the railway companies, the working expenses on the traffic being on a low scale.

The other case was that of train loads of grain in bulk worked from port to an inland town a distance of about 45 miles—also in competition with a waterway, for which a very low rate (less than half the normal figure) was given in respect of the large train load quantities. In this case 12 ton wagons were provided, 50 wagons to a train, and each train load consisted of 600 tons of paying traffic: that was the quantity condition which secured the special train load rate. Here again no doubt such a concentrated and heavy load constituted a very distinctly paying proposition; and a comparison with the average train loads on British railways given on page 25 enables us the better to appreciate its significance.

There exist in England a good many local illustrations of traffic conveyed by railway at low rates which has been developed or secured to the rails as against water competition by the quotation of very low rates, which has only been rendered possible by the condition that the traffic must be in train load quantities, so as to keep the railway costs down to the minimum.

In the history of British rate-making, the dead meat and provision rate for imported traffic from Liverpool to London (originally 25s. per ton, and in recent years raised to 56s. per ton) has played a large part, and also come in for much criticism. This 25s. rate from Liverpool to London was applied originally to dead meat (imported) in train loads of 26 wagons containing 2½ tons each—65 tons per train. Such rate over a distance of 200 miles gives a train mile receipt of 8s. 1½d.[1]

Mr. Pratt in his book on *The Railway and the Traders* gives some figures as to the total value of the trade in the earlier years of this traffic, and adds an interesting

[1] At the present high rates it would yield 18s. 2½d. per train mile.

account of how attempts, which were not successful, were made to apply similar rates for large quantities to traffic originating in the home country. But whilst other experiments have been unsuccessful, the Liverpool-London special rate has been extended to many additional commodities.

It would appear from what has been said that specially reduced rates for traffic conveyed in large quantities might play a very important part in traffic development, but it would seem as though the sound policy were to apply them in specific instances where circumstances call for special treatment, rather than to apply a train load scale all round. Such rates have never been recognised in English railway rates schedule, in any general manner, excepting in so far as the rates for mineral class (i.e. for coal, coke, limestone, ironstone and iron ore) may be considered to be subject to low figures because they embrace traffic which nornally is conveyed in train load quantities.

The view against a general recognition of train load rates was adopted when the rates legislation took place in 1891, for the parliamentary committee, which ultimately determined the rates schedules yielded to the strong representations which were made against the adoption of train load rates for coal, and refused to embody the principle of train load rates on the statute book. The draft orders as introduced by the Board of Trade in the first instance in their bill, which set out the rates that railway companies were to be allowed to charge, provided for train load rates for coal traffic when 250 tons were sent at a time. Thus, as a sample, the proposed maximum rates from Wigan to London were to be 7s. per ton for 10-ton quantities, 7s. 2d. per ton for smaller quantities, but 6s. 8d. per ton for train load quantities of 250 tons at a time. But the opposition to any such reduction of rate on large quantities on the ground of its giving an undue advantage to the large dealer as compared with the smaller merchant was so determined when the question came before the parliamentary committee that the proposal was dropped.

There is not, however, in England any judicial or

statutory pronouncement [1] against train load rates (as there is in America), and it is for the goods manager of any company to consider as each individual application comes before him whether the conditions or circumstances of a large and regular quantity justify the quotation of an exceptional low rate.

Following the Regulation of Railways Act of 1894, which requires the railway companies themselves to justify any increase of conveyance charges they may think proper to propose, there was a general pronouncement by the Railway Commissioners that any such increase of rate or charge, if it is to be substantiated, must have its foundation in *an increased cost* of facilities or of train working; and if this is the expressed and generally accepted view of the determining tribunal, it would seem to be a consistent view that a condition of train load quantities constituted a fair basis for a reduction of the conveyance charge, for there can hardly be any question but that a considerable saving in the working cost per ton results when traffic is handed to the railway company in train load quantities; and if cost of working be taken as the main item on which to base rates, the principle of reduction for train load quantities would have to be admitted as a just one. But it is clear there are other important considerations to take into account, and there is no doubt much wisdom in limiting quantity reductions to car loads or wagon loads. The question of charges, however, is not the one we are discussing in these chapters; we may be content to conclude by acknowledging the far-sightedness of a president of a large trunk line in America who insisted, "First load well your cars, then the trains will take care of themselves."

In the United States the legislature has been much more specific in its pronouncement against train load rates as such than in our own country. The basis of political justice

[1] Sir William Acworth has, since the First Edition of this book, drawn my attention to a decision in 1874 in the case of the Ruabon Coal Co. before the Court of Common Pleas in favour of train load rates. This was nearly fifty years ago, but, although it is nearly fifty years ago, it ought perhaps to be quoted as well as the action of the Parliamentary Committee of 1891 referred to in the preceding paragraph.

in the American constitution is the explicit equality of every man before the law, and the accepted legal view of that country appears to be that to give a reduced rate for conveyance of any specific traffic in train load quantities is equivalent to an undue preference to the big merchant as against the smaller, and in that land of equality such preferential treatment is not to be tolerated.

The Interstate Commerce Commission has actually registered its pronouncement against the principle as being one of unfair "discrimination" on behalf of the larger as against the smaller trader. The case on which this decision was given was that of a railway which had quoted a rebate of 5d. a ton in consideration of a trader sending 30,000 tons in a year, distributed in lots of 250 tons, to be forwarded five times every fortnight.

The Interstate Commerce Commission in giving judgment against any such arrangement, said:—

"A discrimination such as this offer and its acceptance by one or more dealers would create, must have a necessary tendency to destroy the business of small dealers. Under the evidence in this case it appears almost certain that this destruction would result, the margin for private and wholesale dealings in coal being so small. *The discrimination is therefore unjust within the meaning of the law.* It cannot be supported by the circumstance that the offer is open to all. Although made to all, it is not possible that all should accept. A railroad company has no right by any discrimination not grounded in reason to put any single dealer, whether a large dealer or a small dealer, to any such destructive disadvantage."

CHAPTER II

THE GROSS TRAIN LOAD

THE last chapter was intended to make quite clear the distinction between the net freight train load and the gross train load. We mentioned the case of a train load of 50 wagons of grain whereof the gross load was 920 tons and the freight load 600 tons, the tare ratio being 35 per cent. In an empty train the tare weight is the gross load (the freight load would be nil), the gross load being the sum of the wagons without any freight; the tare ratio in such cases is therefore 100 per cent. Assuming for the moment that the grain train selected for example represents the high-water mark of goods train loading from the point of view of tare ratio, then the tare ratio may vary at any figure within the range of 35 to 100 per cent. It is the operating officer's business to be on the constant *qui vive* to keep this tare ratio at the lowest possible level.

It is worth while to again bring to the fore Mossop's figures quoted in the last chapter as to the relation between average freight load, average gross load, and average and maximum capacity of engines. The figures were given for the N.E.R. They were :—

	Year 1910.
Average freight load	126·5 tons
Average gross load	362·8 ,,
Average engine capacity	671 ,,
Maximum engine capacity at—	
20 m.p.h.	1,215 ,,
15 m.p.h.	1,350 ,,

RATIOS.

Freight load to gross load, 35 per cent.
Gross load to engine capacity, 55 per cent.
Engine capacity—average in relation to maximum, from 50 to 55 per cent.

It is the gross train load we are dealing with in this chapter—the actual weight of the train from the point of view of the locomotive, if the expression may be allowed—the aggregate weight of the loaded wagons, that is, which the engine does or can haul.

And this brings us at once to a point of some importance, namely, that we must distinguish between what an engine can haul—that is its tractive capacity—and what it does in pratice haul day by day—the tonnage load it is set to pull when coupled on to a train, viz. the weight of the wagons and contents behind the engine and tender, measured in tons. Of the tractive power or capacity of the locomotive we shall deal in our next chapter.

As yet British railways do not compile or publish statistical records of gross train loads. Such figures, however, are now published in regard to American railroads, and railway operating officers in the U.S.A. are encouraged to watch this development with a view to maintaining as good a relationship as possible between capacity and actual performance.

Let us now go back to the illustration of a typical good mixed freight train given on page 20, and we may note that the gross load here was 61 wagons and 718¾ tons. This would require a heavy engine—probably of 1,000 tons tractive capacity—to negotiate, for a locomotive must always have a margin of power beyond what is called into play. A mixed train load is always a variable factor, and in this particular case it may have been noticed there were 8 wagons out of the 61 which had not more than 2 tons load. If the average wagon contents had been increased 20 per cent., the gross load would have risen 789 tons; and if the engine had been a smaller one, say of 750 tons hauling capacity, its capacity would have been exceeded and a certain number of wagons would have had to be left behind.

Let us put down in tabular form the tonnage, gross weight of the load of the three trains (grain, iron segments, and mixed freight) referred to in our last chapter along with three or four other trains illustrative of varying types :—

Description of Train.	Tare Weight of Wagons in Tons.	Weight of Traffic Contents in Tons.	Gross Weight of Train (adding 20 Tons for Van).
50 wagons bulk grain—port to mill ..	300	600	920
45 wagons tube segments—Stockton to London	247½	360	627½
61 wagons miscellaneous freight train ..	368	350¾	738¾
N.E.R. electric hauled coal train (40 wagons)—Shildon to Middlesborough	350	800	1,170
G.W.R. mixed freight train (96 wagons) —Severn Tunnel to London.. ..	510	960	1,490
L. & Y. 100 wagon coal empties ex Goole	575	—	595

These loads are all typical of freight trains regularly running in traffic to-day, and make one wonder whether Mossop's figures of 1910—an average gross load of 363—would not be much higher to-day (if we could know the precise figure) either on the N.E.R. or as the average of all the British railways.

It is certain that such loads as that given for the N.E.R. of 1,170, or for the G.W.R. as 1,490, would by our forefathers of a generation ago have been described as amongst the impossible attainments under the limitations of our locomotives and gauges. But—I think it was Oliver Cromwell who was responsible for the saying—" The chief glory and enjoyment of life is in doing things that are impossible," and that which is beyond the attainment of one generation often becomes the common practice of the next.

I suppose a load of 7,500 tons as a practical attainment in America would only a few years ago have been considered an impossibility, and yet that is what to-day constitutes the regular load in working iron ore over the Great Northern Railway between the mines in the Missabe Range and Duluth. This was, I believe, until two or three years ago, the maximum gross train load in the U.S.A. A few other noteworthy samples of big loads in that marvellous country of the West are given below :—

3,250 tons gross load. Coal trains from the Pocahontas Coalfields (12 trains per day) by the Norfolk and Western

R.R. (over a heavy gradient portion of this track, where pusher engines are now used, electric power is being substituted for steam working).

4,500 to 5,000 tons. The Chicago, Burlington and Quincy R.R. haul trains of coal from Herron, Illinois, to St. Paul, Minnesota, a distance of 600 miles.

5,000 tons. Coal trains from West Virginia to Norfolk Va. Virginia R.R.

5,000—6,000 tons. Baltimore and Ohio R.R. work trains of this tonnage from Chicago Junction, Ohio, to Chicago, Illinois, a distance of 275 miles.

Commencing in 1920, much heavier loads are being worked on the Virginian Railway, where coal trains of 9,000 tons are commonly hauled ; and recently an experimental train of 15,400 tons (American or " short " tons) was worked from West Virginia mines to the seaboard. The train was over a mile long, but is reported to have been successfully manipulated so far as the locomotive was concerned ; 76 per cent. of its weight was paying freight.

The operating officer in England may well stand aghast as he contemplates such figures as are here referred to as obtaining in America. But his function is not that of trying to attain to American standards, but to try and improve working conditions at home: and the figures given are sufficient to show that without any attempt at sensational developments the working officers have a wide margin to work upon and within which to effect improvement.

Let us now refer to one or two companies' working instructions in regard to the loads which may be hauled by freight locomotives on their respective lines ; and we will take two northern railway companies, both of whom handle a large proportion of mineral traffic, the former L. & Y. and N.E.R. Companies. The primary instruction of the former company on this subject is : " The maximum load of merchandise train over the L. & Y. railway is 1,000 tons. The length of train must not exceed 120 wagons, including brake van." From Goole to Wakefield is one of the most favourable sections of line as regards gradients in the kingdom, and here the L. & Y. Company worked their heaviest freight loads. The limitations of load in actual working are set out below, the figures of load being in respect of an average speed of 15 miles per hour; the variations of load over the different sections into which the piece of line is divided are necessary because of the varying grades.

Gradient No.	Section of Line.	Class of Engine. "Coal" Group. Tons.	Class of Engine. "A" Group. Tons.
1	Goole to Whitley Bridge	1,000	700
2	Whitley Bridge to Knottingley	800	500
3	Knottingley Depot West to Knottingley Station	800	500
4	Askern to Knottingley	1,000	700
5	Knottingley to Pontefract	800	500
6	Pontefract to Methley Junction	940	600
7	Pontefract to Crofton Junction	800	500
8	Crofton Junction to Wakefield	950	600

These loads are diminished by about 20 per cent. for trains which are required to be run at a greater speed, i.e. up to 20 miles per hour, and by about 40 per cent. if the speed allowed is 25 miles per hour.

The whole of the former L. & Y. system is sectionised and tabulated in this way, and these instructions are issued and laid down to enable all concerned in the train working to make up train loads according to the tonnage given for the section of line over which a train has to travel.

This method of arranging the train loads also indicates at once to the driver and guard whether or not they are conveying the maximum tonnage for the particular section of line over which they are working.

The train load is regarded as of such importance that the company have instituted through their "control" organisation a card system of recording the load conveyed by each individual train over sections of the line which have been carefully selected, and by this means it can readily be seen at any time of the day what trains are passing over these sections of the line and the load in tons which they are conveying. At the close of each twenty-four hours the particulars from these cards are transferred to other cards, and by this means the loading of each individual train throughout its whole journey can be ascertained daily, and further, by this method of watching the trains the individual load of every train can be followed, and as a matter of fact, where trains are regularly running, their loading record is available for years past.

One important company, recognising the importance of obtaining good train loads wherever possible, has instituted a system of analysing the traffic which arises on its line with the primary object of ascertaining where through full train loads are presenting, so that arrangements can be made to work the traffic in through trains, and thus obtain the advantage of full train loads, whilst at the same time avoiding unnecessary intermediate marshalling.

Still, however, the more common way to show the loads of engines (we might call it the traditional method of our home railways) is by tabulating the loads in number of wagons. The engines' loads are given in manner set out below. I take this from a book of working instructions.

ENGINE LOADS IN NUMBER OF WAGONS.

Section of Line.	Class A Engine.				Class B Engine.				Class C Engine.			
	Mineral.		Goods.		Mineral.		Goods.		Mineral.		Goods.	
	Up.	Down.	Up.	Down.	Up.	Down.	Up.	Down.	Up.	Down.	Up.	Down.
A to B ..	35	32	35	32	35	32	35	32	35	32	35	32
B to C ..	32	32	40	40	21	21	30	30	18	18	26	26
C to D ..	40	38	40	40	29	25	40	35	25	22	35	31

This is the method in which the goods trains loads are usually shown in the load regulations on British railways, except by a few companies who have commenced to educate their train staff to calculate their loads in tons.

On one of the main trunk lines of England the load limitations are thus shown :—

Section.	Class of Ordinary Goods Engine. (Tank or Tender.)	Load in Wagons.		
		Coal Train.	Goods Train.	Empties.
A to B	2–6–0	50	60	60
	2–6–2	60	80	100
	2–8–0	72	85	100

NOTE.—1½ empty wagons equal 1 loaded goods.
2 empty wagons equal 1 loaded coal.

Here it will be seen a note is added as to the equivalent number of empty wagons to be calculated as "one loaded goods" or "one loaded coal"; and now that wagons have grown so largely in size, these "equivalent" tables for calculation of the larger type of wagons are becoming more and more complex and embarrassing. But these adjustments do not make for accuracy.

On every section of railway it is of course necessary to give separate figures for each variation in the type or strength of the locomotive; in the last table set out above the wheel classification of engines has been adopted on the same lines as are being adopted for engine classification in the companies' yearly reports: this nomenclature will be fully considered when we come to deal with the tractive capacities of locomotives.

I propose to further illustrate the meaning of the gross train load in its application to practical working on the North Eastern Railway, a railway with which I am more familiar than any of the others. The table on the following page indicates train loads which are typical of what North Eastern goods engines are doing with goods train loads; the illustrations are taken from the "Loads of Engines" instruction book in operation on the railway.

All these loads are the scheduled figures of the haulage capacity at the two speeds given of the most powerful N.E.R. freight engines over the sections named for goods trains (not mineral); an illustration of such an engine will be found facing page 48. It will be noticed that the limit of load in this table is 1,000 tons, this being for goods trains. It should be pointed out that the North Eastern is very favourably placed in having some long runs over level country, giving these heavy engines scope for very good performances. The variation in load in the above table depends of course upon the factors of grade and curves on the sections dealt with.

Section of Line.	Distance in Miles.	Load in Tons.	
		At 20 m.p.h.	At 25 m.p.h.
Hull to Gascoigne Wood	35½	1,000	900
York to Darlington	44¼	1,000	900
York to Newcastle	79½	—	745
York to Scarborough	42	840	755
Hull to Leeds	48	650	585

It is important next to note that the figures of load limit given above are for *goods* trains. The same engines when in mineral service drawing coal trains can haul an additional tonnage equivalent to 10, 15, or 20 per cent.[1] increase on the goods tonnage figures.

I set out below the maximum loads of mineral trains on four sections of the North Eastern Railway, taking certain sections which can be compared with the table of goods train loads given above, and including the three principal sections of the N.E.R. heavy coal train working, viz.: (1) Stella Gill to Tyne Dock, (2) Shildon to Middlesborough (Newport), (3) Gascoigne Wood (Yorkshire Collieries) to Hull.

MINERAL LOADS (IN TONS) ON THE N.E.R.

Section of Line.	Distance in Miles.	At 15 Miles per Hour.
Stella Gill to Tyne Dock	10¾	1,300 (if 75 per cent. is in large capacity wagons)
Shildon to Newport ..	19	1,130 (if in 10½ ton wagons)
Gascoigne Wood to Hull.	35½	{ 1,125 (20 miles per hour) 1,000 (25 miles per hour)
York to Scarborough ..	42	{ 935 (20 miles per hour) 840 (25 miles per hour)

[1] Varies according to grade and other characteristics of section of line.

The question at once arises, Why can a heavier load of mineral traffic be worked by the same engine than when the load is composed of goods. And the answer to this question is important. The explanation is that a mineral load is *more concentrated,* that is, it is carried in fewer wagons, on fewer axles, and in a shorter length of train.

When a load is thus concentrated, there is less resistance per ton than in a longer train of the same total tonnage, or, putting the same fact another way round, an engine of any given hauling capacity can haul a larger load the more highly that load is concentrated, which concentration involves its being carried on fewer axles. A very little reflection is necessary in order to appreciate the reasons for this.

1. The longer the train, the greater is the resistance from friction of wheel flanges on the rails when going round curves.
2. The greater is the surface exposed to the resistance of side winds.
3. The longer the train, the larger is the number of wagon axles, every one of which is a point of resistance.

Coal and iron ore, being extensive as well as heavy traffics, are taken as typical of concentrated loads. A grain train with loaded wagons with 12 tons of grain per wagon would come within the definition of concentrated load, or indeed any traffic that averages heavy wagon loads.

The North Eastern definition of a concentrated load as set out in their "Loads of Engines" book is as follows :—

> Every train where the average freight load is 7 tons or upwards per wagon is a concentrated load.

Within this definition, therefore, would come not only coal and ironwork, but grain traffic loaded as described on page 21. All these are "mineral or concentrated" loads.

As we remember the effect of a concentrated load in the increase of the haulage capacity of the engine, we get a better understanding of the importance of high capacity wagons in a direction that is not always present to our thoughts. But the experience which various railway companies have had in the use of 15-, 20-, and 40-ton wagons has given emphatic confirmation to the reality of this advantage, and of the gain in effective engine power.

As the size of wagon is an important factor in its effect on the concentration of load of a mineral train, I here give the following table to show the advantage in increased contents or paying freight in various classes of wagon as actually worked on the N.E.R. system. The so-called 20-ton wagon is plated to carry 23 tons, and when it is filled with small coal (a large part of which is little more than coal dust) it can easily convey 23 tons in practice, and I have therefore taken that figure for the contents weight in this comparison :—

ENGINE CAPACITY, SAY 600 TONS.

	Gross Weight of Train.	No. of Wagons.	Total Weight.		Tare per Wagon.	Percentage of Paying Load.
			Freight.	Tare.		
					T. C. Q.	
In 10½-ton wagons	606	36	378	228	6 7 0	62·4
In 20-ton wagons	599	18	414	185	10 5 0	69·12
In 40-ton wagons	616	11	440	176	16 0 0	71·4

It will be interesting to see the effect upon revenue receipts of this improved wagon loading through the adoption of the larger wagon unit, and we can easily make a comparison by assuming the receipt in coal to be 1d. per ton per mile. Then over a journey of 50 miles we should get for three separate trains hauled by an engine of exactly equal capacity and for conveyance in a train of exactly similar gross weight the following revenue earnings :—

COAL TRAIN OF 600 TONS GROSS WEIGHT.

	Load.	Receipts.
If conveyed in 10-ton wagons	378 tons	£78 15 0
If conveyed in 20-ton wagons	414 tons	£86 5 0
If conveyed in 40-ton wagons	440 tons	£91 13 4

This represents the relative traffic values of a train load of similar traffic where the only alteration is one of the character of the wagon carrying the traffic, the aggregate weight or load of train being practically the same in the three cases; but owing to the load in 20-ton wagons (the second line of the statement) being much shorter in length and carried on fewer axles, the engine could haul probably 10 or 15 per cent. more in load.

The tabulated statement which has been already given of the train loads running on certain sections of lines in the North of England have been selected as illustrative of the largest and heaviest class of the freight engines in service, but in practice, of course, the engines vary, and the loads are graded for the varying classes of engines. If we take, for instance, one of the main lines of the system, that between York and Normanton, we find the load capacity figures given for five varieties or classes of engine at the three speeds of 15, 20, and 25 miles per hour are as set out below :—

Goods Train Engine Loads (York and Normanton).

	Engine Types.				
	C & R.	P.	P_1.	P_2 & P_3.	T.
Class A trains, 25 m.p.h. ..	440	—	—	—	—
Class B trains, 20 m.p.h. ..	585	610	675	745	900
Class C trains, 15 m.p.h. ..	650	680	750	825	1,000
Mineral or Concentrated Loads—					
At 25 m.p.h.	490	—	—	—	—
At 20 m.p.h.	650	680	750	875	1,000
At 15 m.p.h.	715	750	825	905	1,125

Before bringing to a conclusion this chapter on the gross train load I should like to emphasise the importance of an all-round effort to educate the responsible railway servants in the practice of reckoning train loads in tons. It is the only accurate way in which comparisons can be made or loads stated ; and now that high capacity wagons are coming increasingly into play it becomes essential. This may mean something of a revolution in the whole system of British practice in this matter, but it goes to the root of this question of load improvement. The method of calculating freight train loads in tons had been begun on several of the principal railway systems when the war broke out, but, like so many other developments, received a severe and serious set-back when the war absorbed all our best energies : we may believe that one of the features of the new era in the railway world will be the more general adoption of tonnage measurement in estimating our freight train loads.

The goods guard of the future must be a man who is familiar with the tonnage standards, and will know every day as he goes home at night, or at the conclusion of his eight hours' shift, exactly how many tons he has been instrumental in moving during the day ; and as he reflects upon a record tonnage that he has moved, he will be able at the end of his day to " go down to his house justified " in a sense that he cannot do to-day, for he never knows as long as he calculates a train load in wagons only whether his freight load is really satisfactory or larger than normal.

Experience, moreover, goes to show that loads will increase almost, so to speak, automatically when those in charge of train working are really measuring accurately the loads they are dealing with. For precise knowledge always leads to progress, just as the converse is also true that progress is retarded wherever the darkness of ignorance prevails. This question will be again referred to when the guard's journal is dealt with in a later chapter.

Some prominence was given to this question of the importance of knowing accurately the train load in a report of the Board of Trade inspector upon an accident which occurred in the North of England in 1918, particulars of which are recorded in the blue book report of railway accidents for that year. The case was that of a collision with serious consequences owing to the overloading of a goods train when apparently *neither driver nor guard knew that the train was overloaded.* The fact was brought out at the inquiry that the train load was 370 tons 17 cwt.—40 tons in excess of the maximum accepted by the staff, the custom and practice prevailing being, as admitted by the guard, to limit the load to *25 vehicles and the brake van,* irrespective of the gross weight. The guard stated that he had never been accustomed to work to the tonnage loading given in his Appendix rules; it had always been his practice to work to the number of wagons. In the case of the goods train in question the load consisted of 15-, 12-, and 10-ton wagons, which the instructions provided were to be taken as the equivalent of 20, 15 and 14 tons respectively. According to regular practice the train was not considered to be overloaded, although in fact it had an excess of 40 tons in weight.

Whilst so far we have been dealing with the freight train load only, it would perhaps be desirable that we should give some figures as to the gross load of passenger trains, so that a general comparison may be kept in mind. With passenger trains, however, an important point to remember is that the power of the engine is required for speed rather than for the hauling of heavy loads. The exigencies of war requirements have put upon both freight and passenger engines burdens which are considerably beyond the limit which a few years ago one would have thought they could comfortably bear. It is now a not uncommon matter for a passenger train to Scotland, or on the Great Western main route between London, Bristol, and Plymouth to load up to 500 or even (in the height of a busy season) 600 tons. Further details of these passenger loads will be found in the next chapter.

It is one of the most important principles in train working that a locomotive should always have its train "well in hand," by which is meant that it should always have a margin of capacity for hauling beyond what is called for in its daily performances, and it must be remembered that all descriptions of weather have to be provided for. The steady increase in the size of train loads means therefore that there is a constant demand on the ingenuity of the engine builder to improve the design and increase the power of the locomotive; of this we propose to treat in our next chapter.

CHAPTER III

THE TRACTIVE CAPACITIES OF LOCOMOTIVES

It will probably occur to many readers that a chapter with this title ought rather to be written by a trained engineer—by one who understands the locomotive on its technical side, who knows how to measure its powers and how best to enlarge its tractive power when necessary.

But there is perhaps advantage otherwise ; for the great army of railway operators whose function it is to make use of the engine power provided by the mechanical engineer are more interested in the practical results in haulage capacity arising out of the employment of the engines than in the calculated ratios and the mechanical relations between the working, or as they are technically called "reciprocating," parts of the machine.

It is of the practical factors and the limitations that affect the results that we are now to speak—of all those factors in the natural order of things which must have serious consideration by anyone who is to employ a locomotive to best advantage, and obtain from it its best work. For the degree of a locomotive's achievement depends entirely upon how it can at the moment be adapted to its outward environment of physical circumstance including the very variable factor of weather and atmospheric condition.

If we are told, for instance, simply that the capacity of a locomotive for tractive purposes is 1,000 tons, we must assume that this is for fair weather conditions on a smooth or level grade. If instead of being on the level road the locomotive has to operate on a 1 in 100 gradient, or if the weather be wet, rendering rails greasy, the 1,000 tons capacity may drop at once to 900 or less. The conditions of environment and operation therefore are all important.

I have already referred in Chapter I to a grain train of 920 tons gross load as constituting a good sample load. This train left its impress on the writer's mind, for he had never before realised so forcibly the limits of the locomotive, the difficulties to be overcome, and the elasticity of the theoretic load capacity, as when under the responsibility of authorising the running of this train. The biggest engine available at the time was commandeered: it was an 8-coupled goods locomotive, with a tractive capacity of 1,000 tons, which seemed enough and to spare for a 920-ton load.

But let me recount all the difficulties of this unusual working. The grain, imported, had to be carried in bulk, and neither dock nor railway appliances were normally fitted for this method of handling, so a portable elevator had to be requisitioned to transport the grain from ship to wagon. Then, having selected the best available wagons (covered or box wagons with a capacity of 12 tons each), all cracks and crevices had to be stuffed up, or a proportion of the grain might have been scattered as food for the birds by the roadside as the train proceeded on its journey. Other difficulties to be thought of were: were the wagon couplings and draw-gear strong enough for such a strain? Would the weight be too much for any of the wagon journals? Would the brakes hold in case of emergency? Needless to say all these factors were put to a severe test, nor does the writer forget how, after the first train had been worked through, the inspector in charge came next day to report that, as the weather had been bad and the rails were a little greasy, he had had an anxious moment as he was nearing the top of the one "bank" *en route*—a long but not steep rise—the load seemed as if it were going to prove too much for the engine, and realising that if the train had come to a stand on the incline the brake power might possibly have been insufficient in the unfavourable condition of the rails, he had fearsome visions of what the consequences of a run-away on the wrong road might have been. However, with a struggle the engine overcame, and the load was drawn securely over the summit; and several trains of like heavy load were subsequently worked.

It is well to rehearse these difficulties, for any general

Fig. 1.—British Freight Train Engine. L. and N.W.R., 0—8—0 Type.

improvement in train load achievement can only be accomplished in the face of the difficulties which experience reveals—some smaller, some larger. For England 920 tons gross load is a good load for goods traffic, and makes a good practical starting-point in the consideration of the question of locomotive capacity; for we must have some starting-point, and the average gross train load of English goods trains is not a published or as yet available factor.

The engine used for this piece of work was one of the most powerful goods engines in England to-day—the class known as 0–8–0, an eight-wheel-coupled engine; this type is being standardised as one of our principal heavy load locomotives. The 10-wheel coupled engines, now used to some extent on the Continent and in America, are only in the stage of experiment in England.

Of this class of eight-wheel-coupled engine (0–8–0, 0–8–2, or 2–8–0) all the principal English railway companies have now quite a large number in use; the annual reports set out the number of locomotives classified under each arrangement of wheels, and from these reports we find that on December 31, 1922, the following are the number of these engines now at work:—

Company.	No. of 8-Wheel-Coupled Locomotives. 31/12/1922.
London and North Western	931
Great Western	228
North Eastern	240
Great Northern	127
Great Central	242
London and South Western	4
Caledonian	14

The two illustrations shown (Figs. 1 and 3) represent a modern type of this freight engine in use in England and in the U.S.A. respectively for the heavy class of mineral trains. The illustrations are engines of the London and North Western Railway and of the New York Central and Hudson River Railroad.

It has been a matter of common observation during war

time that a great increase in the size of English trains, both passenger and goods, has taken place. I suppose, had one entered a large engine shed at an important railway centre before the war and asked the shed foreman as to the capacity of his biggest engines, he would have suggested for a passenger engine 300 tons, or even up to 400, and for a goods train 800 or 900 tons. But as the war developed and the number of engines available grew less, it became a common matter on our principal main lines to work 450 or even up to 600 tons on passenger trains and on freight trains even up to 1,400 or 1,500 tons. The table on page 36 sets out some of these gross loads of freight trains.

In America, it will have been gathered from what has been already said, the load capacity of the locomotive has been developed considerably beyond anything we know of in this country. The tabulated records and statistics, not only of revenue receipts and expenditure and of rolling stock and permanent way equipment, but also of work done, and of types of rolling stock, are published in America by the Interstate Commerce Commission, and are very complete in character ; they include a very useful classified summary of their locomotives, an extract from which is set out in Fig. 2 on opposite page.

The figures are taken as at June 30, 1914, and are an extract from the full return, but this table gives the principal designs. (These figures are not now shown annually in this graphic form.)

Design "A" it will be seen represents the arrangement of wheels in which *the whole weight of the engine is on the coupled wheels,* all wheels bearing their proportion of the driving weight, and A2, A3, and A4 indicate the number of pairs of driving wheels on which the weight is carried.

A5, for instance, is a 5-pair or 10-wheel coupled engine, the "Decapod," and of this type there were 23 running in America on the date taken ; whilst of the 8-coupled (the type which I have referred to as in the ascendant for heavy loads in England) there were in America 293 as against no less than 7,696 locomotives of the 6-coupled type. It is not only interesting but useful to see the facts as to locomotive design on the other side of the ocean presented in this graphic manner.

The B type includes all engines with a *pair of leading wheels in front of the driving wheels*, but without "trailing" wheels; and here also we have B2, B3, or B4, according

FIG. 2—UNITED STATES OF AMERICA—CLASSIFICATION OF LOCOMOTIVES.

Single Expansion Locomotives—June 30, 1914.

Short Description of Engine.	Wheel Arrangement.	No. of Locos.	Average Tractive Force per Load.	Total.	Weight on Drivers.
			Lb.	Tons.	Tons.
A 2	OO	476	17,527	41	41
A 3	OOO	7,696	26,829	63	63
A 4	OOOO	293	36,077	81	81
A 5	OOOOO	23	57,135	122	122
B 2	OOo→	3	10,646	27	22
B 3	OOOo→	4,838	24,006	64	55
B 4 (Consolidation) ..	OOOOo→	19,704	37,985	93	82
C 2	OOoo→	7,155	15,904	51	34
C 3	OOOoo→	10,375	24,386	72	56
C 4	OOOOoo→	709	37,874	93	78
D 3	oOOO→	9	20,342	58	44
E 2	oOOo→	9	13,033	44	29
E 3 (Prairie)	oOOOo→	1,364	32,407	101	73
E 4 (Mikado)	oOOOOo→	3,237	51,716	140	108
E 5	oOOOOOo→	42	63,952	152	127
F 2 (Atlantic) ..	oOOoo→	1,737	23,952	91	53
F 3 (Pacific)	oOOOoo→	3,715	33,064	119	77
G 3	ooOOO→	1	12,500	35	29
H 3	ooOOOo→	23	21,894	77	50
J 1	ooOoo→	1	4,675	21	13
K 3	oooOOOo→	18	26,800	120	68

to the number of pairs of wheels coupled for driving purposes.

As regards the 8-coupled engines with a pair of leading wheels, it should be noticed that the principal type in America is the 2–8–0, of which there were over 19,000, as against only 4,838 of the 2–6–0; the pair of leading (uncoupled) wheels being evidently considered a necessity in America for this class of engine for the proper balance and support of the heavy boiler which this engine must carry. The 2–8–0 type of engine is characterised as B4.

The "Atlantic" type 4–4–2, now so well known in England as a passenger engine, is, it will be noticed, identified as F2, and there were (June 30, 1914) no less than 1,737 of these engines at work in the States—a most popular type of passenger engine; but it is surpassed in number by the "Pacific," or 4–6–2, called in this classification F3, of which there are 3,715. Of the 4–6–0 type of passenger engine there are over 10,000.

I have in an earlier chapter referred to the difference in point of view between the locomotive superintendent and the traffic officer or operator on this question of the power or tractive efficiency of the engine. The traffic officer in his anxiety to get bigger train loads finds it very easy to press his mechanical colleagues to build a larger proportion of larger and stronger engines; but the engineer in view of the figures of difference between actual load and engine capacities on any test of averages, has at present an effective retort in asking the traffic operator to make better use of the engine power he already possesses. The friendly criticism between these parties is stimulating, and so long as each is ready to see the other's point of view, is healthy and helpful, for are not both officers working to attain the same end—more economical working? It is at this point when discussion from different points of view is being entered upon that statistical records of the attainments of past years are, where they exist, so helpful. That train loads in England have increased there can be no doubt, but to what extent only accurate figures can help us to gauge; and one of the firmest and soundest of bases on which to estimate the requirements and possibilities of the future is to be found in the study of accurate and precise records of past attainments. Meantime we are, I think, justified in anticipating that a larger proportion of heavy engines will be necessitated in the future as a policy of larger loads and heavier trains continues to be pursued.

In giving illustrations of the practical capacity of loco-

Fig. 3.—American Freight Train Engine. New York Central Lines. 2—8—2 Type.

motives, we have already pointed out that the element of speed is one of importance ; and that a high capacity locomotive which can take a load of 1,000 tons at 20 miles per hour may have to be reduced to 900 tons or less, if an average speed of 25 miles per hour is expected of it. For an ordinary goods engine available for mixed loads of an average character, it is convenient to give the capacity in three alternatives at 15, 20, and 25 miles respectively.[1] Fast dead meat, milk, or fish trains run at passenger speeds are equipped with efficient brake power applied by the engine driver, whilst the ordinary goods train, limited to slower speeds, has no continuous brake at work, and is dependent for stopping upon the driver's brake power on the engine wheels, supplemented by the guard's hand-brake on his van wheels. The speed which is allowed for a goods train is in large measure governed by its power of stopping (i.e. its brake power) rather than by the engine's tractive capacity for hauling the train.

We may now consider the important difference between a passenger and a goods train engine. It *is* an important difference, although—and this sounds rather paradoxical—the difference between passenger and goods engines when we come to detail seems to be fading away, or at least to be much less than it used to be ; for the passenger train of to-day has attained to such a degree of size, that is of weight, that it equals or surpasses the maximum goods train weight of a generation ago, and a correspondingly heavy engine of enlarged tractive power is therefore necessary.

Let us explain, however, in more detail what has been happening in the evolution of the type of locomotive with the growth of heavy loads. I remember well being told in my earlier days in the railway service that a goods engine was easily distinguishable by the fact that it had six driving wheels coupled together. At that time the "crack" fast speed passenger engine was Stirling's single driver on the G.N.R. which used to haul the principal East Coast trains between London (King's Cross) and York. The other express

[1] These are shown differently by different companies in their working instructions, varying according to circumstances, but these three gradations are commonly adopted.

passenger engines were 4-coupled, such as the L. & N.W., until quite recently supplied almost entirely for the haulage of the West Coast trains over their line. But with the advent of the "Claughton" class of engine (6-coupled) on the L. & N.W.R., the 4-coupled drivers are to an increasing extent "taking a back seat," and within the last year or two the remaining Great Northern uncoupled single wheelers have actually been placed on the scrap-heap. Now the contest for primary place in passenger working lies between the Atlantic type (4–4–2), which has four coupled driving wheels preceded by a leading bogie or truck on four smaller wheels, and followed by a pair of trailing wheels to help carry the heavy weight of the boiler and superstructure of the engine, and the 6-coupled engine (4–6–0) with a leading bogie, but no trailing pair. The very heavy fast express trains are being worked to-day by these two types, 4–6–0 and 4–4–2, and one or two companies are experimenting with a larger type, 4–6–2.[1]

The 6-wheeled or 8-wheeled coupled engines are now used for main line and heavy freight trains, and the coupled driving wheels may or may not be preceded by a pair of leading wheels or by a 4-wheeled bogie or truck. The 4–6–2 type is usually used for fast goods train running, so that the 6-wheeled-driver engine in this way becomes either a passenger or a fast goods train engine.

The railway companies' annual reports and the Ministry of Transport published annual railway returns give a statement of the number of types of locomotives owned by each company, and the Railway Accounts and Returns Act of 1911 requires that the "wheel types" of locomotives are to be set out in the returns rendered. The classification of engines as between passenger and goods which used to be given effect to in the railway half-yearly (now yearly) reports has now been abandoned by almost all railway companies. The important distinction in principle, however, remains that a passenger engine is built primarily for speed,

[1] Since the above was first written, Mr. Gresley's 4–6–2 locomotives have been doing excellent work with passenger trains between King's Cross and Grantham, and Sir V. L. Raven has just completed a similar type engine for N.E.R. main line working. Photographs of the former and of an "Atlantic" type are shown in Figs. 4 and 5.

FIG. 4.—BRITISH "PACIFIC" (G.N.R.) PASSENGER ENGINE, 4—6—2 TYPE.

whilst a goods engine is built with its first object that of hauling a heavy load.

To compare with such figures as we have given of maximum heavy goods train gross loads going up to 1,350 tons in the case of the North Eastern, and 1,500 tons in the case of the Great Western, we set out the tonnage loads in the case of some of the principal passenger trains of England which illustrate the 500 or 600 tons to which reference has been made :—

Company.	Train.	No. of Carriages.	Aggregate Tonnage Weight of Train.
Great Western ..	Cornish Riviera Express	15	508
L. & N.W.	Euston–Liverpool Express	15	490
G.N. & N.E.R. ..	East Coast Express	19	583

A passenger engine for the heavy main line work in these days must therefore have a capacity of hauling 550 or 600 tons, and at an average speed of at least 60 miles per hour on the level road. Nor must the rule for efficient working which has already been enunciated be forgotten, viz. that a locomotive engine should always have a capacity a little beyond the requirement of its normal work. The station master or traffic operator in times of an unexpected rush of traffic is under severe pressure to put on an extra coach, but it is very important that he should remember the limitation of maximum capacity of the engine. If it is overloaded, it will lose time on its journey ; and it has never seemed to the writer quite fair upon the mechanical engineer to expect him to haul loads with his engines considerably beyond what he has specifically indicated as the maximum capacity of the machine.

Although we are dealing with the *capacities* of locomotives, their limitations are also important, and it is well that the traffic operating officer should have this aspect of the matter continuously in mind. The locomotive engineer may feel—especially with the advent of electric traction—that the rail locomotive has still almost unlimited possibilities in tractive power in front of it, and that limitations to its performances come from " other departments " ; but the local superintendent must realise the limitations. These limitations are various. The responsibility may be with the permanent way engineer, whose bridges or roadway are not strong enough for the larger loads, or who is restricted by the dimensions of loading gauge ; or with the traffic superintendent, who does not load up the trains to what the engine can take if given the chance. Then there is the clerk of the weather, whose provisions seriously affect and often limit the train loads : to this influence we shall refer again. It is not at the moment our desire to apportion blame upon any particular section of the personnel : we want to face up in a spirit of dispassionate inquiry to the true facts of the situation.

We must not leave out of account in our enthusiasm to bring down the cost of working, which undoubtedly is materially reduced per ton of traffic as average loads are increased, that considerable extra cost is caused by these heavy trains in such directions as :—

1. Extension of relief siding accommodation.
2. Stronger wagon couplings.
3. More efficient brake power.
4. Stronger bridges and permanent way.

There are in the cost of these factors very practical limitations to continuous increase in size of locomotives, and to each of these factors much consideration must necessarily be given. They, equally with the savings achieved, must be measured up and recorded.

The technical business of a locomotive is the overcoming of resistances to its forward motion, and the principal of these resistances it will now be well to mention. The size of load is perhaps the first factor ; but that we have already dealt with in some detail. Other resistances are due to—(1) gradient against the load ; (2) axle resistance through friction ; (3) frictional resistance at the point where rail and flanges of wheel come into contact ; (4) resistance due to head wind or a heavy side wind blowing against the surface of the train ; (5) resistances due to the internal arrangement of reciprocating parts or to some flaw in structure of parts. The latter is so entirely technical and mechanical

Fig. 5.—British "Atlantic" (N.E.R.) Passenger Engine, 4—4—2 Type.

that it does not come within the scope of this book. Of the other resistances we shall have something to say one by one.

Grade Resistance.—This will depend on the degree of grade (i.e. steepness of acclivity) and the length of the climb; for a short length of upward grade—say a quarter of a mile at 1 in 100 or a half-mile at 1 in 200—the momentum of the train, if going at a speed of 30 miles an hour, should "carry on" with such further "pull" as the engine can exert; but if the up grade continues, the load will have to be reduced as compared with the engine load on level ground. The gradient is the severest of all limitations, as the locomotive is then pulling against the natural force of gravity.

Resistance due to Curves.—This resistance is very considerable, and especially with long trains. The longer the train the greater the number of contact points where frictional resistance occurs, and the resistance becomes cumulative. So that a 400-ton train (gross) carried in 15 wagons would offer considerably less resistance than the same weight of train spread over 30 or 40 wagons. This is the case of the "concentrated" as compared with the more diffused load to which subject we have already drawn attention in the chapter on gross train loads.

Frictional Resistance at the Axle.—This is also a most important resistance; the whole train load—the "rolling" load, that is—falls upon the wagon axles, and every axle offers the resistance of friction. So here again, as with the wheel flanges on curves, the resistance is cumulative, increasing with the number of contact points. In this case also comes great advantage with concentrated loads as the load is then borne on fewer axles.

And lubrication is all important. In this connection the weather tells with great effect. It is found in practice that loads have always to be reduced in cold weather, and this is mainly due to the effect of temperature on the oil or grease used for lubrication. It may be taken for granted that in warm weather an engine can haul at least from 10 to 20 per cent. more in load than in cold weather; and for the same reason the load resistance is much less after a train has been running than when it starts from inertia. That the axles "warm up" to their work is no mere empty phrase, for as soon as they become warm the frictional resistance is greatly reduced.

In this connection we would set out one or two of the practical instructions which exist in the companies' books of regulations to trainmen as to weather conditions :—

The instruction under this head in the case of one railway is as follows :—

> "The load is to be reduced at the discretion of the yardmaster or person in charge during unfavourable running conditions, such as frost, snow, heavy wind, or greasy rails, etc."

And another :—

> "In windy, frosty, and slippery weather the loads must be arranged in accordance with the information supplied by the enginemen as to what his engine can take and keep time with."

In practice the calculated figures as to limitations in load, speed, etc., are on the assumption of fair average weather. When specially bad winds, rain or snow prevail, allowances have to be made by the person in charge—the driver, the yardmaster, or the train foreman, as the case may be.

In this chapter I have used the term "tractive capacity" to indicate the capacity in tonnage load which the locomotive is designed in practice to haul. Theoretically the tractive power of an engine is obtained by an engineering formula which gives the proportion of the weight on the driving-wheels which is available for haulage after the balance has been absorbed in rail adhesion. It is found in practice to be from 20 to 25 per cent. of the total weight of the engine ; thus an "Atlantic" (4–4–2) engine, whose total weight was 90 tons, with 48 tons weight on drivers, would absorb 36 to 38½ tons in adhesion, and have 9½ to 12 tons available for "drawbar pull" or haulage effort against resistance of the train. This pull on the drawbar is the "tractive power" of the engine. Its relation to the total weight on the driving wheels of the locomotive is dependent on the steam pressure, the cylinder dimensions, and the wheel diameters; the variation between 20 and 25 per cent. being dependent upon a right relationship between the different parts named.

The laws which determine the coefficient of friction or the general resistance of the load of a train to the locomotive power as indicated in the engine drawbar pull are very complex, but I venture to put down some of the practical effects of these laws as shown by observed facts.

1. Loaded cars have far less resistance per ton than unloaded or empty cars, and concentrated than diffused trains loads.

2. The resistance is greater at starting in the case of a goods train (though the velocity resistance is practically nil) than when it is travelling at 8, 10, or 15 miles an hour.

If for instance the resistance is 20 lb. per ton at starting, it may drop to less than half this figure at 10 miles per hour.

3. Journal (i.e. that portion of the axle which passes through the axle box of a wagon) resistances are very greatly reduced by higher temperature, insomuch that increasing velocity (owing to the warming of journals and bearings) tends to neutralise any additional resistance due to the higher speed; and this results in the aggregate resistance of a goods train remaining more or less constant over a long range of low velocities, say from 7 to 20 miles per hour.

4. At a given speed the resistance due to journal friction is less if the speed has just been reduced from a higher one than if it has just been increased from a lower.

5. In the winter months the general results in the way of movement of trains on a railway system are considerably below those of the summer months, as the effect of the bad weather increases the resistances both of wheels and journals; the load capacity of the engine may have to be reduced in cold or greasy weather by anything from 5 up to 20 per cent. Cold and frosty weather prevents normal lubrication, and snow or continuous moisture on the rails tends to

promote "slipping" of wheels on rails, or in other words reduces their normal power of grip.

In our next chapter we shall consider some of these phenomena from the driver's point of view.

CHAPTER IV

THE DRIVER'S REPORT

We now come to consider the function of the document known as the "Driver's Report" or "Driver's Ticket." It is known by various names as used by different railway companies, such as "Daily Report of Driver," "Driver's Journal," "Driver's Ticket." In this chapter we will use the term "driver's report" for short title to distinguish it from the guard's "journal," which we shall deal with in our next chapter. Every driver is required to give a daily account of his stewardship, how many tons or wagons he has hauled, how much coal he has burned, etc., etc. We will subsequently analyse one of these reports, two samples of which are set out (Figs. 6 and 7).

It is well we should recognise that an engine-driver in his daily work is rendering service to the community; not only is he earning his wages, but he is in a very direct way adding to the stock of wealth in the country—the true economic function of the human unit. If we take such a case as a driver of a fish train from Plymouth to London, it is easy to realise this; the fish is of little value at Plymouth, in London it has a greatly enhanced value. It needs to be transported from Plymouth to London, whose population needs it, to turn it into wealth. The driver does not usually live in the consciousness of the fact that he is doing national service of a higher character, but in that he is adding to the wealth of the country, he is truly so engaged, and it is a matter of real importance that this aspect should not be overlooked. An enlightened driver will look beyond the fact that he is "earning his wages," or even that he is keeping his engine in order, and will remember that every citizen who is in any real sense *earning* his wages is a true patriot rendering national service. Of this service the driver's report gives a full analysis day by day.

It may be as you look through a file of driver's reports you think you can imagine hardly anything more wholly dull, uninteresting, and routine in character; but if you can realise what is behind the ticket—that it is but the documentary evidence of effective service of the driver, and that it provides information which when aggregated in statistical form is of vital importance in management, the dry documents may be indued with a new interest, and appear, as they are, an essential part of the living railway organism.

Kirkman, an American writer and railway officer, states in one of his books that perhaps there is no single thing in railway working more important than the locomotive, and recognising the truth of this, as I think we may—for the locomotive represents the power which leads to movement, the great feature of all transport—we must agree further that the driver is an important railway servant.

The fact that every company requires from its drivers a statement day by day of the work each man has been doing, and requires it in much detail, is evidence of the importance attaching to the work—the service he performs; and the high standard of wage he receives is in harmony, too, with the recognised importance of his work.

A locomotive driver's duty may be at the outset divided into—(1) the mechanical side, which requires that his engine be supervised and kept in good working condition; (2) the service rendered, which impels him to get as good work out of his engine as he can.

It is the second function that is day by day committed to writing in the "report," and it is highly important that we should understand the nature of that document and what is exactly its *raison d'être.*

We shall find the document is varied in its form according as it is used by different railway companies and goes by different names. The different blank forms are headed: "The Driver's Daily Return of Work Performed"; or, "The Engine Driver's Daily Return" (G.E.R.); or simply (this is the L. & N.W. Company's designation), "The Driver's Ticket."

In different ways the following information is asked for and recorded in regard to the driver or his work :—

The time he went on duty.
The time he came off duty.
The time he started with his train.
The time he finished with his train.
The number of hours he worked and requires to be paid for.
How terminal time (i.e. time occupied before and after being in charge of his train) was employed.
Between what points he was working.
How late or punctual his train was at all important points of the journey.
What load he conveyed.
How many full and how many empty wagons.
How many miles he ran.
How much shunting work he performed during the day.
Particulars of any lodging allowances or other out-of-pocket expenses.
Particulars of relief provided or assistance rendered by other engines.
How much coal, water, oil, etc., he has consumed during the day.

Whilst the forms vary, they all require an accurate statement of the miles run, and we may summarise the function of the forms by saying that their most important service is to get at a record of the miles run, the loads worked, and the fuel consumed: we have included the loads worked as being amongst the requirements of the driver's reports (although the keeping of this record is primarily the duty of the guard), and in this chapter propose to devote some attention to the consideration of how in practice the driver is expected to calculate his load.

The driver knows the rating of his engine capacity in tons (we dwelt on this in Chapter II). How does he calculate the tonnage he is handling? The answer to this question brings us face to face with one of our great needs in railway operating—the need of a better system of calculating loads. As a rule we find that the driver has no means of calculating, and can only make quite a vague estimate. Usually the method of computation is somewhat as follows : Engine capacity 600 tons, i.e., roughly speaking, 60 goods or 40 mineral wagons, and the driver reflects, "I must take care my load *in wagons* does not exceed that figure."

With certain exceptions to-day (which will be dealt with hereafter), all the loads of trains are reckoned in number of wagons (or carriages for passenger trains), and it is the guard's duty to furnish the driver with the " make up " of the train required in number of vehicles.

In addition to the driver's ticket and the guard's journal, some companies adopt a third form for the guard to use on which to record the number of wagons or carriages for the driver's information. In these cases the driver is charged with the duty of providing himself with a supply of these forms, and of handing a copy to the guard before he leaves his home station, which form the guard has to fill up and return to the driver as soon as the latter uncouples from his train at the end of the day. This is a good practice, and obviates the possibility of any mistake in the verbal transmission (which is so easy) of figures from one man to the other, and any difficulties arising from discrepancy in figures between one and the other. A copy of this form is set out on page 68 (Fig. 8).

Where the traffic is of uniform weight or density per wagon, as in the case of a mineral train, it matters comparatively little for the daily work of the driver and guard whether the load be counted up in wagons or tons, because the gross wagon weight is in these cases fixed and definite ; but from the point of view of general information, or for any scientific consideration or statistical use of the figures, the tonnage computation is almost essential, and in these cases it is as easy, granted a knowledge of the multiplication table, to reckon in tons as in wagons.

Let us now imagine that the same driver with his 1,000-ton capacity engine is one day for some reason—it may be promotion to a higher grade engine—transferred to a new or different link where the wagon loads vary greatly, and the problem he has to deal with is a very different one. He may perhaps be transferred to a main line general goods train. Here he will find the wagons, as regards their own tare weight, may be anything from 4½ to 9 tons, and even more in the case of exceptional wagons, and the load may vary from nil to 12 tons (or even higher still in the case of wagons for special commodities such as boilers), and if a high capacity wagon of coal or ironstone be included amongst the "miscellaneous," the load may be of 20 or even more tons.

How is a guard, for the purpose of advising the driver, going to reckon all these varying weights of wagon and freight traffic with such a sample load as is for instance set out on page 20? A process of counting is the only true answer, and it falls upon the guard (who is the primary custodian of the train) to have to work out the addition sum involved. Between the driver and guard there must be close co-operation. Let us assume that the driver is offered by the guard, when he is ready to start with his main line goods train a slip (or return) which shows 50 wagons somewhat as follows :—

Section A to E Wagons on Train.	Load Tons.	Tare Tons.	Total Tons.
10 empties	—	55	55
20 wagons with 8-ton load ..	160	130	290
10 wagons with 10-ton load ..	100	65	165
10 wagons with 3-ton load ..	30	50	80
50 wagons	290	300	590

Let us assume further that the engine capacity (for the section from "A" to "E") is 575 tons. Now, with a load of 590 offered, what is the driver's position? Clearly, on an accurate or precise interpretation of his instructions, 3 or 4 wagons would have to be left behind; but *if weather conditions are entirely favourable* and the circumstances seem to demand it, an enterprising driver will risk a few tons over weight.

But now it is time we were examining the details of the form of the report actually in operation. The blank form is necessarily a little complicated, for not only has it to record a great number of details which vary in character according to the particular type train it refers to, but it will sometimes relate to one single (or return) trip only, whilst very often, in the case of short distance working, it may have to record three or four (or more) return trips in its day's work. But we shall find certain general features common to every driver's report. In the specimen form (Fig. 6) at the end of the book, and headed A.—— B.—— Railway, it will be noticed that the main portion of the document is an actual explanation of the train work, including a comparison between the appointed or booked times and the actual running record, with columns to fill up setting out the number of vehicles attached to each train and explaining in detail the reasons of any detentions—whether (*a*) by signals ; (*b*) waiting for load ; (*c*) locomotive duties ; or (*d*) from other causes ; a column to record the number of miles run on each trip and columns giving full particulars of the vehicles (number and description) hauled on the train.

Then in another section of the document there is provision for particulars of a variety of duties, services, and circumstances, such as: amount of coal received, water provided when away from the home line, particulars of any time absorbed in shunting, whether in attaching or detaching vehicles, that is, as part of the normal work in dealing with the train or "regular pilot" work (that is, performing shunting services), which would naturally and under normal conditions be performed not by the train engine, but by a shunting or pilot engine told off for the purpose. This division of the time spent in shunting as between the engine's normal work in connection with its own train and general shunting of wagons in the marshalling or station yard is an important distinction, and in the statistical returns is separately classified.

As the driver's report form varies considerably between different railway companies, we have set out at the end of the book a second form (Fig. 7) ; it is of a more modern character, and is included because it makes provision for the train load being shown in a tonnage figure. A comparative study of these two forms will be found interesting. On the C.—— D.——

Railway form columns are provided to specify the amount of time absorbed in "shunting," "standing in steam," and "locomotive duties" respectively, whilst on the back of the return special provision is made for—(1) explanation of any detentions, (2) remarks as to any special incident or occurrence, and (3) an analysis of the time occupied in shunting. In the centre of the front side of the report is a column which asks for the "gross tonnage of the train, including working van." This item of the tonnage load is furnished to the driver by the guard.

The calculation of tonnage weight is usually provided for by the provision of a separate form known as the "Guard's statement for driver." The principal columns in this form are those which record the aggregate weight of the wagons as they leave each station. To obtain this aggregate weight the guard must at some stage of his journey make out a list of the wagons and the weight, including the contents of each. We shall deal with this in our next chapter on "The Guard's Journal." A copy of the form here referred to ("Guard's statement for driver") is set out (Fig. 8) on page 68. One company requires a weekly return from drivers : it has the advantage of letting a driver take a *résumé* of his week's work before he sends the return away. The greater interest of figures comes when they can be used for comparative purposes, and a record such as the following :—

Monday ..	800 tons	Thursday ..	900 tons
Tuesday ..	862 ,,	Friday	820 ,,
Wednesday ..	1,012 ,,	Saturday.. ..	840 ,,

enables the driver to pick out from the week's work the day on which he made, so to speak, the biggest achievement in his week's work ; and supposing the 1,012 tons hauled on the Wednesday was the highest record ever made by his engine, this particular week will have in the driver's mind and in his engine's record an extra interest as a red-letter day. Statistics become illuminating when they reveal progress, and as they enable comparisons to be intelligently made.

In the case illustrated on page 65 of 50 wagons of

Guard's Statement for Driver.—MERCHANDISE TRAIN.

Date. Commencing on________________191___ Ending on________________191___

Engine No._______. Class__________. Belonging to__________________Station.

Engineman's Name__________________Home Station__________________

Place Stopped or Engaged at.	TRAIN TIME.						LOADED WAGONS.				EMPTY WAGONS.			Total Wagons (Loaded & Empty)	Total Tons leaving each Station, including Break.	Maximum Tonnage laid down.	TIME.			
	Train due out from Starting Point.		Arrival.		Departure.		Goods.	Cattle.	Coal.	Other Minerals.	Goods.	Cattle.	Minerals.				Shunting.		Stationary.✱	
	H.	M.	H.	M.	H.	M.											H.	M.	H.	M.

This statement must be accurately filled up and signed by the Goods Guard up to the time of his giving up duty, and then by the shunter or other person in charge (should the Engine do any work after the Goods Guard leaves it), showing the time occupied in standing and shunting, and at what time released to go to Shed.

✱ **All standing time by the Engine must be shown in this column, including the time whilst shunted for trains to pass, signal delays, or detentions from other causes.**

*Signature of Goods Guard*________________ *Home Station*________________

*Signature of Shunter*________________ *Home Station*________________

Fig. 8.—Guard's Statement for Driver, Merchandise Train.

varying weights and loads, if the load had been simply estimated in wagons, the real weight of the train might easily have been put down as 30 tons short of the engine's capacity, or 30 tons more than its tabled capacity, without the driver being in the least aware of the fact.

If the system of computing loads in wagons is permanently continued, it will be essential to make a great number of special calculations and computations to adjust the larger wagons to a common standard, as to-day, for instance, we find on one company's system not only is there the rule that three wagons of goods or four empties must be reckoned as equal to two mineral wagons, but there is a somewhat elaborate table of adjustments such as—

Five coke wagons equal 4 mineral wagons.
Five 10-ton mineral equal 6 ordinary mineral wagons.
Of 12-ton wagons 8 equal 11.
Of 15-ton wagons 3 equal 5 if loaded, 2 if empty.
A 30-ton wagon equals 3 ordinary wagons.

We may reasonably conclude that any driver or guard who has these adjustments to make will really find it easier to reckon each wagon and its load in actual tons, *if only he has the means of doing it*, and a tonnage standard gives him the means of comparing train with train, which the variable unit of "wagon" will not do.

A driver knows the haulage capacity of his engine in tons (each driver presumably knows the capacity of his own engine); but unless he has also the means of knowing every week the tonnage which his engine has hauled day by day, he has no means of estimating how much below capacity were his engine performances, or indeed of measuring in any way his locomotive's achievements, in its relation to its traffic work. We return to this subject in our next chapter.

Before concluding we must say a few words to emphasise the importance of an accurate record being kept of the fuel burned and the oil consumed—which some companies' drivers' reports make provision for. The size of the railway companies' coal bills can best be appreciated by the following figures in regard to coal consumption of two companies taken from the Board of Trade Returns for 1913. The reader may make his own adjustment as to the present day cost value corresponding to these pre-war figures :—

COAL CONSUMPTION BY TWO RAILWAY COMPANIES IN 1913.

	Company "A."	Company "B."
Cost of coal one year	£1,160,041	£900,172
Total engine miles	48,000,000	44,600,000
Cost per mile	5·8d.	4·84d.
Number of locomotives	3,084	3,019
Coal cost per locomotive	£376	£289
Miles per locomotive	15,576	14,776

From these figures it would appear *prima facie* that the coal consumption on railway "A" is much worse than on railway "B," but it may be that railway "A" can more than justify the increase compared with "B" by showing a lesser coal consumption per gross ton mile. Further, one company may be conveying a high class of important traffic necessitating high speed, whereas the other company might be mainly concerned in the conveyance of slower moving traffic. Assuming, however, the traffic of the two companies to be more or less equal, the figures would show a field for the exercise of economy in the consumption of coal on the part of Company "A" especially when it is remembered that a by no means small proportion of the calorific power latent in the coal disappears through leakage during combustion ; and great is the difference sometimes discovered between driver and driver in their power of economising with fuel, and getting the most effective service from the locomotive with the least expenditure and cost.

Various are the methods that have been adopted for encouraging or persuading the drivers to be economical in the use of fuel and oil. In olden days a coal-saving bonus was offered to drivers as an inducement towards economy ; but this inducement was abandoned as resulting too often in a reduction not only of the coal consumed, but also in the engine's effective daily work.

Publicity amongst the drivers on the various sections or "links" of the consumption of coal by different engines which are doing similar work is found to be one of the best methods of inducing drivers to practise and cultivate economy in coal consumption. Below is set out one of the returns of coal consumption on a specific main line link of 17 drivers in which it will be seen that those drivers whose engines have consumed more than the average consumed by all the engines on the link have the attention of everybody concerned drawn to the fact. The return is for one week or one month, as the case may be.

MAIN LINE ENGINE WORKING COAL CONSUMPTION—LINK OF 17 ENGINES.

Week ending............1920.

Name of Driver.	Number of Engine.	Coal Consumed per Mile.	Excess over Average.	Excess over Lowest.
		lbs.	lbs.	lbs.
A. B.	1234	28·4	—	—
C. D.	5678	31·3	—	2·9
E. F.	910	31·7	—	3·3
*	*	32·1	—	3·7
*	*	32·4	—	4·0
*	*	33·0	—	4·6
*	*	33·8	—	5·4
*	*	34·6	—	6·2
*	*	35·8	0·7	7·4
*	*	35·9	0·8	7·5
*	*	36·3	1·2	7·9
*	*	36·4	1·3	8·0
*	*	37·6	2·5	9·2
*	*	39·0	3·9	10·6
B. A.	1243	39·2	4·1	10·8
B. C.	1342	39·5	4·4	11·1
B. D.	1432	41·2	6·1	12·8
Average 17 engines		35·1	—	—

As the actual work of the engines must vary not a little in any given month, and this work (the loads hauled and trips made by the engines) is not dependent on the driver, it will not do to write down a man as extravagant or wasteful merely because he has a heavy consumption measured in lbs. per mile. He may have had exceptional loads to haul. If some measure of the work performed, as for instance the gross ton miles hauled by the engines, could be also recorded in these published sheets it is clear that they would be of considerable additional value. Gross ton miles not being available for specific lines, the consumption of coal by freight engines per 100 wagon miles run would afford some indication of the effective work of the locomotive from a coal-burning point of view.

We must not forget to give to the fireman his due in connection with the fuel economy question. It is a common saying in the American railway world that the true fireman is born, not made, so great is the difference between the skilled man and the mere routine worker.

The amount of steam power obtained out of a given quantity of coal will depend largely upon care in stoking and feeding the fire-box. I have seen a notice exhibited in an American round-house or engine shed, reading :—

> " Enginemen and firemen must work together so as to save coal and reduce smoke. The burning of bituminous coal in a locomotive engine requires air, which must be admitted through the grates and through the fire door. Smoke means waste of coal and must be avoided. Large quantities of coal placed at one time in the fire-box cool down the fire, cause smoke and waste coal ; the best result is obtained from small quantities at regular intervals."

In this matter of the careful and economical use of coal the chief responsibility falls on the stoker or fireman, and there is much advantage in the regular practice on British railways of having the grade of driver recruited from the ranks of the firemen, for he is thus by experience trained to supervise the work of his fireman ; and whilst he, the driver, is held fully responsible for the care, conduct, and performance of his engine, yet absolute co-operation between himself and his fireman is essential.

It may be said that the three attainments which stand first in contributing to the success of a driver's work are :—

1. Knowledge of his machine on the mechanical side.
2. Power to measure in definite terms the result of his engine's effort.
3. Ability to supervise the fireman and his work.

It would be easy to become eloquent in any attempt to summarise the duties of an engine-driver. Each locomotive has its peculiarities, and it is the business of a driver to thoroughly understand his machine. The more complicated the machine and the more varied its requirements, the greater the necessity for adaptability on the part of the driver. A driver must be full of resource ; he must be able to understand the engine's foibles and to fathom its peculiar secrets. The driver who telegraphs home in his difficulty on the road, "My engine is disabled ; what am I to do ?" is not ideal ; he will have to give way to others.

The functions of a driver require constant watchfulness. He must examine his engine before starting ; he must see that the tools are on the engine, that he has a proper supply of coal ; a tank full of water ; that sand is in the sand-box ; that his engine is clean. He must examine the outside gear, the boiler for leaks, and the condition of grates and oil-cups, etc. He must know the rules of the road and the signals, and he must take note as he travels of any unusual occurrence during his journey. Finally, let us remember there are always two classes of men : those who have an ingrained love for the facing of difficulties and know no higher joy than that of overcoming ; and secondly, those who never rise to this higher vision, but whose main thought during the day is to finish their task and go home. These latter have no worthy place, and fortunately are seldom found, amongst British engine-drivers.

CHAPTER V

THE GUARD'S JOURNAL

As the driver is required to tabulate the record of his engine's daily performances, so the guard, whether passenger or goods, has to make out his daily record of the work of the train of which he is in charge, these two functionaries, driver and guard, being directly concerned in the transport of goods from point to point.

The traffic load of a train, whether alive or dead, is in charge of the guard, but for one reason or another this responsibility of custody is more readily recognised in the case of passengers, luggage, live stock, and small parcels carried in the van, than in the ordinary descriptions of goods or mineral traffic conveyed by goods trains.

The journal which every guard is required to fill up daily varies as between differing companies, and sample passenger and goods train journals are set out in Figs. 9 and 10, but the principal standard particulars which are required to be recorded in the journal are as set out below :—

Guard's name and where stationed.
The time booked on ; time booked off.
By what engine was train or trains worked.
Time due to depart from starting station.
Actual time started.
Time due to arrive at destination.
Actual time arrived, giving minutes late.
Particulars of load of train.
Times of arrival and departure at every stopping place.
Vehicles attached and detached at each point *en route.*

Identity numbers of each carriage and number of wagons.

In case of detention, reasons for delay to be accurately stated.

State of weather.

The above are the principal standard particulars required of the guard, but necessarily modifications have to be made to suit circumstances of varying railway systems and for adaptation to passenger, goods, or mineral trains.

There is not a little diversity as to the way in which the *loads* of trains are recorded. In the case of passenger vehicles, a common practice is to provide columns for—(1) Actual number of vehicles, (2) Equal to [1], (3) Weight in tons; or simply—(1) No. of vehicles, (2) Weight in tons. (Some companies adopt the simple formula "No. of pairs of wheels," "No. of axles," instead of weight of the train.)

Dining or sleeping saloons and particulars as to attendants will usually require to be specially shown in blank spaces provided for the purpose.

On a main line long-distance passenger train punctual running is the leading feature to which the superintendent attaches main importance. With other descriptions of trains, e.g. short distance coal trains, it may be the feature of load that commands or needs greater attention.

But let us first look more generally at the guard's report from the point of view of the superintendent's office authorities. The district superintendent's office is the repository of all these daily journals. Here they are carefully and critically examined, endorsed, and duly pigeonholed, probably in monthly batches under a file for each train—or at least for all the important trains.

The superintendent, or one of his assistants, goes carefully through the documents, the superintendent himself examining a register of the trains in which the running of each of the more important trains is recorded in tabulated form, so that any continuous record of bad or belated running or any flaw in the timing of any train which inter-

[1] Indicates equivalent in normal vehicles when exceptional vehicles are computed in relation to a standard vehicle.

feres with the smooth and punctual working of the great railway machine may be at once considered with a view to remedy.

It may be found, for instance, that a particular train is reported regularly for many days in the month fifteen to twenty minutes behind time, owing to its scheduled timing clashing with some more important passenger train which must be given precedence. In this case some alteration of the booked time of one or both of the trains clearly should be given effect to. Or it may be found that the train is continuously losing time owing to too heavy a load; then one of some three alternatives will need to be resorted to: either (1) a higher capacity engine must be requisitioned, (2) a restriction of the load may have to be adopted, or (3) a longer time may have to be allowed for the train *en route*. This is a sample of the kind of work which the trains record clerks of the superintendent's office are occupied with. Constant supervision of the "journals" is the principal means the superintendent has of realising how the trains in his division or district are running, and the knowledge that all details of train running are thus constantly before the superintendent is a continuous incentive to both driver and guard to be on the *qui vive* to keep their train to time, and to avoid detentions or anything that militates against the punctual working of the train.

A first principle in all train working is to keep the trains to time and in accordance with scheduled working, and any departure from such booked time, at least if it is more than a minute or two, ought to be a matter for some explanation to the supervising authority. This obtains both with passenger and goods trains, for in the complex machinery of train working each class of train interacts inevitably upon the other. But the passenger trains quite properly always take precedence. For detention to human freight will always have consequences much more directly felt and more loudly expressed than in the case of inanimate goods traffic.

Next in importance to this question of punctuality is the load of the train, and the superintendent needs therefore to watch the loading of the train, the number of carriages or wagons which it has hauled and the tonnage load that the vehicles represent. The train may have one or two extra vehicles on without the engine being overloaded, especially in fine weather, for the normal load in carriages is liable to fluctuate in weight; and as regards goods trains, this fluctuation is much more marked, as the traffic conveyed varies so greatly day by day.

As regards passenger train loading, the guard is occasionally asked to record in his journal the number of passengers travelling by the train. This is, however, not frequent, for it is not easy for the guard to count the passengers, having regard to his other duties, and usually the station masters *en route* or special staff are appointed for the purpose of obtaining this information.

Where wagon miles are recorded, a very effective way of watching the working and achievements of goods train engines is by recording for any section of line where improvement is desired, or any special supervision is considered necessary, the wagon miles negotiated day by day, and setting out these figures in a weekly return. Attention may often be concentrated with great advantage on a specific section where improvement is desired over a period of a few months or even for a year or two.

A sample of such weekly return is set out below, and includes two separate return trips of trains working day by day on the North Eastern Railway :—

Wagon Miles Worked on Booked Goods Trains During Week Ending Sunday, October 9, 1910 : York District.

Date.	9.15 p.m. York to Darlington. Distance 44½ Miles.				7.0 a.m. York to Leeds. Distance 26 Miles.			
	Engine No.	Engine Hours.	Wagon Miles.		Engine No.	Engine Hours.	Wagon Miles.	
			Loaded.	Empty.			Loaded.	Empty.
Out.	P.2.				P.1.			
Monday, 3rd ..	412	12½	1,257	1,744	1988	15	638	415
Tuesday, 4th ..	412	10¾	1,593	1,677	1988	14	238	808
Wednesday, 5th.	412	11¾	516	22,36	1988	14¼	587	775
Thursday, 6th ..	818	12¼	1,034	1,524	1991	12¾	430	293
Friday, 7th ..	412	13	2,774	1,118	1991	12½	565	344
Saturday, 8th ..	412	11	1,677	1,677	1991	14	528	478
Total ..		71½	8,851	9,976		82½	2,986	3,113

Wagon Miles Worked on Booked Goods Trains During Week Ending Sunday 9, 1910: York District—(*Continued*).

Date.	1.20 a.m. Darlington to York. Distance 44½ Miles.				12.15 p.m. Leeds to York. Distance 26 Miles.			
	Engine No.	Engine Hours.	Wagon Miles.		Engine No.	Engine Hours.	Wagon Miles.	
			Loaded.	Empty.			Loaded.	Empty
Home.	P.2.				P.1.			
Monday, 3rd ..	—	—	—	—	1988	—	629	107
Tuesday, 4th ..	412	—	2,680	687	1988	—	683	226
Wednesday, 5th	412	—	2,719	734	1988	—	392	219
Thursday, 6th ..	412	—	2,452	850	1991	—	379	180
Friday, 7th ..	818	—	2,904	482	1991	—	422	67
Saturday, 8th ..	412	—	2,976	357	1991	—	451	265
Sunday, 9th ..	412	—	2,779	826	—	—	—	—
Total ..		—	16,510	3,936	—	—	2,956	1,064

Aggregate wagon miles for the two trips .. 39,273 Wagon miles per engine hour .. .. 549·3	Aggregate wagon miles for the two trips .. 10,119 Wagon miles per engine hour .. 122·7

To the casual reader or student it may well appear that the figures in these tables are too numerous or complex to be of much practical value, but it must be remembered they are only made use of for supervision purposes by a skilled assistant who by long experience has become proficient in the understanding of figures of this kind, so that he is always able and can, often at a glance, determine which particular engine or train's record needs improving or smartening up. From the table of wagon mile records here set out we get the following summary, the results it will be noticed showing considerable variation :—

Wagon Miles in the Week.

Train.	Loaded.	Empty.	Total Aggregate.	Per Engine Hour.
1. 9.15 p.m. York to Darlington and return	25,361	13,912	39,273	549·3
2. 7.0 a.m. York to Leeds and return	5,942	4,177	10,119	122·7

The much fewer number of wagon miles per engine hour obtained in the case of (2) as compared with (1) will no doubt be accounted for either by the different character of the line or by the difference in the work and functions of the train. The smaller wagon mile results obtain with a train which is doing roadside work, stopping at each station to lift or leave wagons, whilst the large figure in the first instance above is the record of a through journey with a good load throughout.

To obtain an effective survey of the work of trains on any section of line dealt with, the trains on that section must be summarised in an aggregate total of wagon miles and compared year by year as is done in the case of the sectionised wagon mile return set out by Mossop (page 46 in his book on *Operating Statistics,* which is here reproduced) :—

Section "A" to "B." Year.	Wagon Miles.		Hours.		Train Miles.		Wagon Miles.	
	Loaded.	Empty.	Train.	Shunting—by Train Engine.	Total.	Per Hour.	Per Train Mile.	Per Train Engine Hour.
1907	1,354,633	1,026,201	6,840	1,300½	45,362	6·63	52·5	292·5
1908	1,348,955	1,142,600	4,550	745	40,308	8·85	61·8	470·6
1909	1,387,731	1,186,155	4,384	709	40,106	9·15	64·2	505·4
1910	1,450,223	1,288,972	4,482	746	41,982	9·37	65·2	524·0

A survey of this summarised table will reveal that a very considerable improvement has been taking place on this particular section of line during the years included in the survey. The load in wagons represented by wagon miles per train mile has grown from 52·5 to 65·2; and the increase in miles per hour of nearly 50 per cent. (i.e. from 6·63 to 9·37) shows conclusively that the increase in load has not been accomplished at any expense of speed, but on the contrary an increase in the rate of movement has accompanied the larger loads. The general increase in the wagon miles per train engine hour shown in the last column of the table is a good index of the all-round improvement that has taken place; and it indicates how this improvement has been a steady factor year by year, though as between 1907 and 1908 the increase was so large that it is quite evident that some new system or complete change of organisation or something quite abnormal must have taken place to affect the figures so largely. But whatever the changes of circumstance or alteration of working arrangements, the effect on the traffic is shown in these figures. They are the measure of the degree of improvement that has taken place. The true function of a summary of figures of this kind is, like the clinical thermometer of a doctor, to indicate progress or the reverse, and the realisation of the fact of progress or improvement is itself a stimulus to further attainment.

The passenger and goods guards' journals and the information called for are set out in full detail in Figs. 9 and 10, pages 82, 83, 84 and 85.

These two forms are selected purposely so as to show something of the variety of detail required in exercising supervision over the running of trains. From the superintendent's point of view hitherto the greatest stress has been laid on the point of punctual running, and very earnest attention has been given to delays and occurrences which have happened and caused train running to be late. In view of the large amount of detention to goods trains (which are always expected to give preference in running to passenger trains), this close supervision is essential, and becomes ever more so as the hours of trainmen become reduced ; but the past method of " taking up " by inquiry forms to station masters and signalmen asking for explanations is a little cumbersome and out of date, apart from being a perpetual source of worry to those who have to rack their brains to try and recall why some two or three weeks ago train No. 238 was detained some twelve or fifteen minutes at the home signal of box No. 3 at West junction—or obtain other accurate information such as the particular inquiry may demand.

The inquiry is natural and easy enough, but ought to be made more promptly than two or three weeks or a month after the event. Necessity is, however, the mother of invention, and the development of telephones and the "control" of train working by constant and continuous 'phone communication with signalmen or station masters through the superintendent's control office is apparently destined to revolutionise these methods of train detention inquiries, and is likely to save much stationery and ink as well as to effect an important saving of time on the part of the superintendent and clerks. The liberation of clerical time and effort which may thus be brought about by improved current watching of the movement of trains may advantageously be directed to another channel which is becoming of increasing importance —that of the traffic load which the train is manipulating.

A scrutiny of the two guards' reports set out will serve to show a number of interesting points of variation which suggest themes for discussion. In the passenger train journal (Fig. 9) the detentions to the train and causes thereof are to be set out in the " Remarks " column, whilst at the foot of the return provision is made for an analysis of the total time lost in the division or section concerned under the heads respectively of " Station work," " Waiting connections at stations," " By signals," " By exceptional causes," " By engineering checks." The size of the load is gauged by a column—in the case of the passenger journal headed " No. of wheels at starting, and on leaving any subsequent station where the load is altered."

In the case of the goods guard's journal (Fig. 10) shown, the principal distinguishing features are that the stations in the first column are printed—a common practice in the case of important main lines—and the " Remarks and occurrences " column (supplemented, if necessary, by a memorandum) is expected to contain all particulars as to train detentions and their causes. The load of the train at starting point and as altered at any station *en route* by vehicles attached or detached must be fully set out (in number of wagons) on the back of the report.

There is no provision in either of these journals for the load in tons. The guard will have to fill up separately the train load in tons for the driver if the latter requires it.

In any event, the guard should know what weight he is carrying on his train ; for the engine capacity is furnished by the locomotive engineer in tons, and it is for both driver and guard to know whether they are exceeding the capacity limit, or if not, how much their load is within the engine's

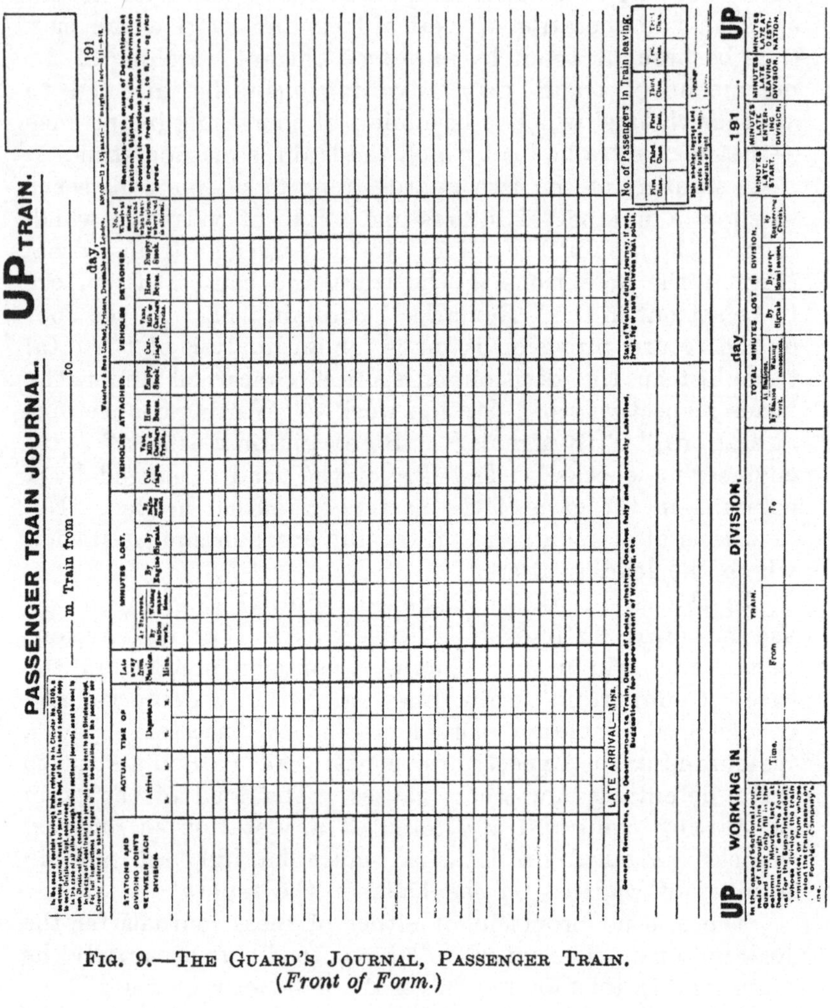
PASSENGER TRAIN JOURNAL. UP TRAIN.

m. Train from ____ to ____ day ____ 191

STATIONS AND DIVIDING POINTS BETWEEN EACH DIVISION. | ACTUAL TIME OF Arrival, Departure | Late away from Station Mins. | MINUTES LOST. | VEHICLES ATTACHED. | VEHICLES DETACHED. | Remarks as to cause of Detentions at Stations, Signals, &c.

LATE ARRIVAL—Mins.

General Remarks, e.g., Occurrences to Train, Causes of Delay, whether Coaches fully and correctly Labelled. Suggestions for Improvement of Working, etc.

State of Weather during Journey; if wet, frost, fog or snow, between which points.

No. of Passengers in Train leaving.

UP WORKING IN ____ DIVISION, ____ day ____ 191 ____ UP

TRAIN. Time. From To | TOTAL MINUTES LOST IN DIVISION. | MINUTES LATE START. | MINUTES LATE ENTERING DIVISION. | MINUTES LATE LEAVING DIVISION. | MINUTES LATE AT DESTINATION.

FIG. 9.—THE GUARD'S JOURNAL, PASSENGER TRAIN.
(Front of Form.)

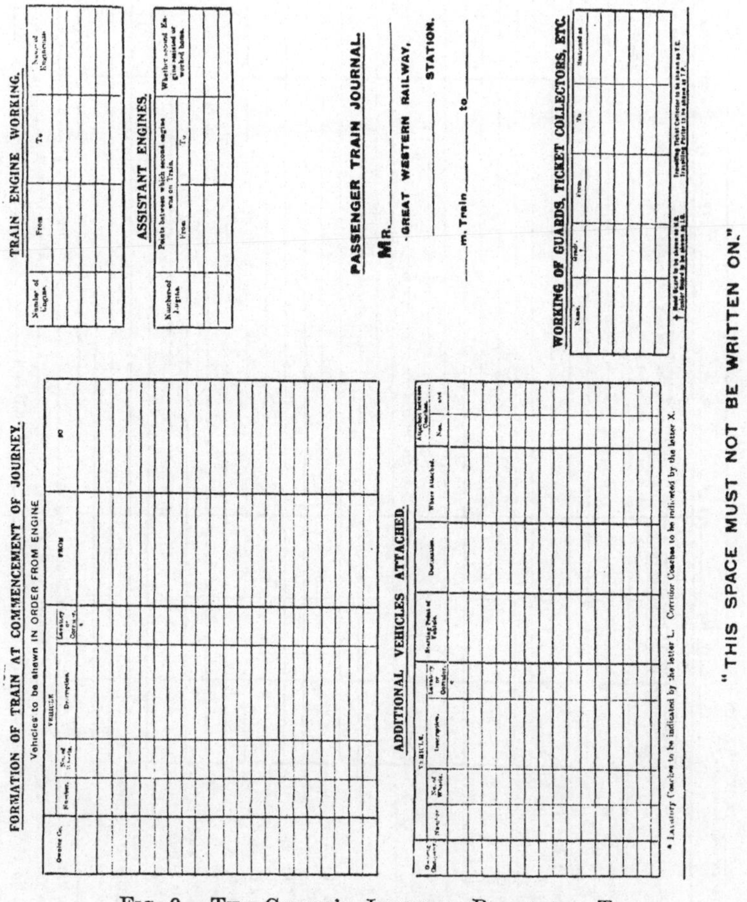

FIG. 9.—THE GUARD'S JOURNAL, PASSENGER TRAIN.
(*Back of Form.*)

LONDON AND READING.

GOODS GUARDS' REPORT.

_______ DOWN TRAIN FROM _______ TO _______
(State the Time, and whether A.M. or P.M.)

_______ *day, the* _______ *day of* _______ 19 _______ M^{c}C. & Co. Ltd., Ldn.

Stations.	Time. Departure Time from each Station as per Service Book.	Actual Time of Arriving at, and Departing from, each Station. Arrived.	Departed.	Remarks and Occurrences. If this space is not sufficient for the whole of Remarks, &c., a separate Memorandum Form to be used, and attached to the Train Report. *State of Weather during Journey* _______	Load below Maximum Load leaving each Station. Trucks. Loaded.	Empty.
Hither Green Sidings						
New Cross (S E. & C.R.)						
London Bridge						
New Cross (L.B. & S.C.)						
Forest Hill						
Norwood Junction						
East Croydon						
Purley						
Coulsdon and Cane Hill						
Merstham						
Red Hill						
Reigate						
Betchworth						
Dorking						
Gomshall						
Chilworth						
Shalford						
Guildford						
Wanborough						
Ash						
Aldershot Camp						
Farnborough						
Blackwater						
Wellington College						
California Siding						
Wokingham						
Earley						
Reading Gas Co.'s Siding						
Reading } Arrive						

No. Brake Van _______ Proper Time of Arrival _______ Before Time, H. _______ M. _______
No. Brake Van _______ Actual Time of Arrival _______ After Time, H. _______ M. _______
The Total No. of Vehicles moved by the Train _______ Head Guard _______ Under Guard _______
Locomotive Engine No. _______ From _______ to _______ Driver _______
Locomotive Engine No. _______ From _______ to _______ Driver _______

See other side for FULL PARTICULARS of the Vehicles *Attached* and *Detached*.

FIG. 10.—THE GUARD'S JOURNAL, GOODS OR MINERAL TRAIN.
(*Front of Form.*)

PARTICULARS OF VEHICLES ATTACHED AND DETACHED.

STATIONS	VEHICLES ATTACHED.						VEHICLES DETACHED.					
	Trucks Loaded with Goods.	Trucks Loaded with Coal.		Empty Trucks.	Various Vehicles.		Trucks Loaded with Goods.	Trucks Loaded with Coal.		Empty Trucks.	Various Vehicles.	
		Ordinary.	15 Ton.		Loaded.	Empty.		Ordinary.	15 Ton.		Loaded.	Empty.
State of Train at Starting ...												
Totals												
Deduct Vehicles Detached ...							Total Number Loaded					
State of Train at end of Journey							Total Number Empty					
							Total Number moved by the Train					

When *assisted* by another Engine, and it is about to be detached, enquire of the Driver thereof where he is bound to, and enter the particulars under the head of "Remarks and Occurrences."
In the case of an Engine breaking down and being replaced by another Engine, state the circumstance, giving the No. of the Engine under the head of "Remarks and Occurrences."
Full particulars of all delays to be included under the head of "Remarks and Occurrences."

Note.—Brakes working the Train not to be included this side.

Fig. 10.—The Guard's Journal, Goods or Mineral Train.
(Back of Form.)

power of haulage. *Only as this figure is known can there be any intelligent understanding of the load problem in its relation to the economical handling of freight trains*—not to say to the safe working of the line. It is of economy rather than of safe working we are speaking in this book. Enhanced efficiency, however, always improves both these factors—economy and safety in working.

The guard of a train, let it be remembered, is the traffic representative in charge of the train, and it is "up to him" to know as much as possible as to the freight of the train whilst it is in his custody. The intelligent guard will always be interested in knowing the contents of the wagons he has charge of as well as the weight which his train carries.

If these words should ever come to the notice of a goods guard, I hope he will at once ask himself the question on how many occasions he has worked a goods train which conveyed 600 tons of paying freight, as recorded in the instance given on page 21, or if he cannot recall the occasion, then what is the nearest he has approached to it.

It must be admitted here that to come up to the standard of efficiency necessary to estimate a train load in tons a guard will have to be required to count. But he is expected to do that already as regards numbers of wagons, and I venture to surmise that the guard who is given to the exercise of his faculty of counting will be a happier man for his attainment and for such exercise even though that exercise be a slight one.

The human unit has been variously described by philosophers as an animal who cooks, who thinks, who laughs, or who worships. I believe one of the truest of definitions if it can be put succinctly by a one verb definition would be rather that he is *the animal who counts.* This counting up of wagons so as to express the load in tons will enable the guard to realise whether his loads are improving, whether they are as good by his train as by his comrade's on his section as a neighbouring section, and interest in his work will grow as he watches and compares.

The goods guard I have suggested should realise that he is custodian of the wagons and their contents whilst they are in course of conveyance by his train, just as a passenger guard is responsible for the custody of the parcels in his van. He must therefore have some system of recording the wagons and their loads, for the workmen cannot work without the necessary tools. The simplest way of providing this is by the system of a wagon-loading card which has been adopted on some lines. It is the application of a card system : to every wagon, as it is loaded, is attached a card ticket as follows :—

A....... B....... C....... RAILWAY.

Goods-Train Loading Card.

......Wagon No.........

From............ To............

Date............ 1923.

Weight of load...........	......tons	......cwts.
Weight of empty wagon ...	......tons	......cwts.
Total weight	......tons	......cwts.

As soon as the loading of any wagon is completed the loader is charged with the duty of attaching the wagon loading card" to the wagon : it can easily be inserted in the ticket clip with the destination ticket. The wagons are turned out ordinarily into the marshalling or despatch sidings, and just before the train starts the guard must see that he has the collected tickets from the wagon clips. He can either pick them up from the wagons himself, or, as is more usual, obtain them from the yard foreman, who tells off a boy for the purpose of furnishing guards of departing trains with their wagon-loading cards. The guard of the train is thus furnished with an inventory of his wagons and their contents, and as he detaches a wagon at a roadside station he hands to the station master on arrival the relative loading card; or if at a junction he breaks up his train into two parts for further conveyance the cards corresponding to each section would be handed over to the guard who is in charge of the trains on each continuing section. So that a guard would always have a loading card in respect of each of his wagons whilst he was on duty. At any time an inspector or foreman coming along and wanting to know the weight of a train could find it from the cards in the guard's custody. The method is simple in the extreme, and with this simple description will, I believe, carry its own commendation.

Anyone who is accustomed to a card system knows its value. Take the case of a library where every volume is indexed on its descriptive card: no better system has been devised than the card system now adopted in all public and institution libraries. If it is found useful and necessary to have a card for every book of value down to 1s. or less, it seems hypercritical to talk of waste of money or labour in adopting a card for a wagon of goods whose value runs into hundreds of pounds. The value of a loaded goods wagon, moreover, is one that grows with the journey. A wagon load of goods is under normal circumstances of greater value at the end of its journey than at the commencement, for it is the very essence and nature of transport to create values. A train is moving goods from a place where they are not wanted to the place where they are needed for consumption and where they are of greater value, and the railway charge for conveyance is, or should be, the larger portion of the difference between the values at the two places.

A train load (say 500 tons) of coal, for instance, at the colliery may represent £250 of value, but when it gets to its destination at port of despatch for abroad, it will have increased in value probably to at least £375; and if the difference was due merely to railway transit, it would represent a rail rate of 5s. per ton.

The method adopted in making up the wagon load tickets or cards undoubtedly requires some consideration, for various grades of the staff will have to co-operate before the system can be brought into operation. This question, as regards goods wagons, is fully dealt with in its appropriate place in the chapter upon the "Organisation of the Goods Station." It has its peculiar difficulties, but they have been overcome in many places, and what man has done in one place man can do in another. I believe that all officers who have adopted this method of recording loads in practice will bear testimony that it more than justifies any labour involved.

Let us revert for a moment to the simple train of 61 wagons set out on page 20: this table is simply a summary of the 61 cards which the guard of the train would have in his pack when this load was being worked—one wagon, one loading card. It may be said that it would prove an unnecessarily cumbersome method for dealing with a coal train for instance whose wagons are all of a uniform weight of 10 tons contents, as the number of wagons in this case at any time gives the load, and the tonnage can at any time be obtained by a simple multiplication. Granting the force of the criticism, however, it is only to admit that for exceptional local working the cards may not be necessary; this criticism of an exceptional case would not vitiate the value of the systematic adoption of the loading card for regular working. It is sure to rapidly grow in extent and in the area of its adoption as the importance of having accurate train load records becomes more widely realised.

Every guard as he travels with his train should have in his custody for reference such a card record of his load as is herein set out.

The possession of such record, as well as constituting an improvement of system, will make the guard himself a more responsible official, as well as a more able and better qualified representative of the traffic department.

A clearer idea of the extent of variation of train loads when reduced to a tonnage standard will be obtained by reference to the statement of weights of some half-dozen heavy freight trains of varying character set out in the chapter on "The Gross Train Load," page 36.

Years ago I remember hearing not uncommonly in discussion derogatory remarks as to the goods guard's duties and the lightness of his job, whose main requirements often appeared to be to jump into his van at the moment of starting and ride in quiet seclusion to the other end of his train journey. I see no point in belittling the duties and responsibilities of a goods guard, or indeed of any grades of railway men. But with more complex working responsibilities must grow and the higher the guard can rise to a sense of his responsibility the better for all concerned.

It has been generally admitted that the guard's position is not so onerous as the driver's, nor so responsible ; and as we set out some of the driver's requirements in the last chapter we may at this point set out the principal duties of the goods guard. The guard may and should look upon his work as a service rendered to the commonwealth along with that of the driver, and that he can by intelligent service contribute not a little in assisting the company which employs him to effect improvement and economies in the working of the goods trains.

A goods guard's duties may be summarised as follows :—

1. To have full custody and responsibility of the train which he has to work and of its freight contents.

2. To see that all the wagon loads are in order and the wagons properly labelled on both sides.

3. To see that wagons are detached at destinations *en route* and pick up others *en route* for conveyance by his train.

4. To keep an accurate record of the running of his train and to fill up and send in daily his "guard's journal."

5. To assist the engine-driver in the application of brake power in the van as required.

6. To keep his van tidy and to take care that all his equipment is in good order (a guard's equipment includes watch, set of flags, 12 detonators, hand lamp, shunting pole, 2 sprags, brake stick, 2 hand scotches, rule-book, general appendix, service time-book or superintendent's programme, and all current notices and instructions).

7. To protect his train in the event of such necessity arising.

8. To see that the van is properly provided with set of side and tail lamps, oil-can, short drawbar, etc.

9. Before starting away with his train to see that tail and side lamps are on the van in their proper places and to exchange signals with the driver.

CHAPTER VI

THE WAGON LOAD

We are to consider in this chapter the question of what is a wagon load? Here again, as with the train load, it may mean either the gross load, i.e. the tare weight of a wagon plus its contents, or it may have reference merely to the traffic contents. It is of the latter we are now going to speak, and we shall use the expression "wagon load" for the contents weight—the freight load of a wagon.

Very considerable attention has been given to this question of the loading of wagons, not only in this country but in most countries of recent years, with the view to, and with the result of, improvement in the size and weight of loads; and fortunately we have now available from the Ministry of Transport a good array of statistics, which will become more and more useful as the years go on and we have a more complete series. There is little doubt, too, that the publication of the figures and the knowledge they convey will *ipso facto*, by drawing attention to the real facts and to the possibility of increase, lead to improvement.

The facts in regard to size of wagon load are very different between British and American or continental railways. Whilst it is with the former we propose mainly to deal and are primarily concerned, it will be well in considering the subject to have some idea of how British wagon loads compare with those in other countries, and I therefore at the outset of this chapter set out some of the facts and figures. We must not forget that the difference of general conditions is of the utmost importance if we begin to make comparison between one country and another.

Whilst in this country we have an average wagon load of between 5 and 6 tons, in America, taking the Pennsylvania

Railroad as an example, the average load per car in 1921 was 31·5 tons. The following is a record of the progress made in the loading of cars on the Pennsylvania Railroad between the years 1903 and 1920 :—

PENNSYLVANIA RAILROAD COMPANY—AVERAGE LOAD OF FREIGHT PER CAR.

Year.	Tons.	Year.	Tons.	Year.	Tons.
1903	23·40	1909	26·81	1915	26·96
1904	23·47	1910	26·82	1916	29·23
1905	24·27	1911	26·59	1917	32·17
1906	25·46	1912	27·45	1918	32·66
1907	27·38	1913	27·86	1919	31·12
1908	26·99	1914	27·71	1920	30·98

These figures include the revenue-earning freight only.

On the face of it, this looks a very satisfactory record of progress in the U.S.A. so far as the wagon load is concerned.

The P.R.R. is by no means exceptional in the record it shows ; and we may give (from the Interstate Commission Report for 1920) the following average wagon load figures for a few of the other principal American Railroad Companies :—

AVERAGE TONS PER WAGON CONVEYED.

Year 1920.

Pennsylvania R.R.	30·98
New York Central and Hudson River R.R. ..	26·02
Baltimore and Ohio R.R.	33·71
Philadelphia and Reading R.R.	37·67
Erie R.R.	27·78
All American Railways, Class I	26·72

In England progress has also been made, and we can give the following figures published by the North Eastern Railway :—

Year.	Average Wagon Load.	Year.	Average Wagon Load.
	Tons.		Tons.
1903	5·11	1911	5·88
1904	5·31	1912	5·79
1905	5·46	1913	No record
1906	5·54	* * *	No record
1907	5·72	1919	No record
1908	5·74	1920	6·12
1909	5·86	1921	5·26
1910	5·87		

The following figures from the Ministry of Transport published statistics give the average wagon load for the principal companies north of the Thames.

WAGON LOADS—PRINCIPAL BRITISH RAILWAY COMPANIES.

Name of Railway.	April 1922. Average Wagon Loads.	
	Total Freight.	Coal Traffic (included in preceding column).
	Tons.	Tons.
All Companies	5·5	8·3
North Eastern	6·3	9·3
Great Central	6·2	8·8
Great Western	6·0	8·5
Midland	5·8	8·2
Great Northern	5·4	8·4
L. & N.W., Northern	4·6	8·0
L. & N.W., Southern	4·9	8·7

The figures in the preceding table are calculated averages: they are given in the published tables, but it is important to point out that there are two units of average load which must be considered by a railway manager or student when dealing with statistics in this country, viz. :—

1. The originating wagon load, i.e. the weight of the merchandise put into the wagon at the commencement of its journey, which is a factor that can be controlled by the railway on whose system the loaded wagons starts its journey. This originating average wagon load may be taken at an individual station for one day or for a week, or for any designated period.

2. The average wagon load over a given period—day or month—of all the loads passing over a particular company's system. This figure includes not only the wagons commencing their journey on the particular system, but also all wagon loads passing over it, or terminating their journey on the system. It is a true average load, and takes account of the variation of load in a wagon on a single journey.

In the latter case it will be realised that the hauling company has, except in the case of wagons starting on its system, little or no control upon the loading of the wagon. To illustrate this point: a fully loaded wagon which starts from a point on the Caledonian Railway Company at Glasgow for Crewe, is hauled from Carlisle to Crewe by the L. & N.W.R. The L. & N.W. Company takes the wagon at Carlisle with the load put into it by the Caledonian Company at Glasgow. Instances do, however, arise where the wagon load at start is not the throughout wagon load. As is pointed out by Mossop in the chapter on "Wagon Loads" in his book on *Railway Operating Statistics*, the "wagon load at start" (i.e. the loading of the wagon at commencement of its journey) is a statistical unit of practical value; but it is not a true average of the load which is hauled over the whole system; the true average wagon load for train operating statistical purposes must take account of any change in the loading of the wagon on its journey. For example, if a wagon starts on a journey of 40 miles with a load of 6 tons of provisions, and at a station half-way on its run sets down half of its load and therefore conveys only 3 tons on the second half of its journey, it is clear that its average load throughout the journey is only $4\frac{1}{2}$ tons, its load at starting point being 6.

The load made at starting point is of prime importance, and the result of even a slight improvement in the average weight per wagon has far reaching effects. One English railway company improved its average load of goods traffic at its principal stations during a period of eleven years to such an extent as to save the haulage of over 1,000,000 wagon journeys in the last year of the period, as compared with the position in the first year of the period. The company were therefore able to carry on their business with a smaller stock of wagons than would have been necessary had their average load remained stationary during the eleven years. They would have fewer trains to haul, greater freedom of their line, and the services of shunting in traffic yards and at goods stations would be greatly reduced, as well as relief afforded at those stations where accommodation is limited.

Further, in the case of this company the better loading of wagons avoided capital expenditure for stock and provision of additional accommodation in sidings and at goods stations.

The "average load hauled" unit is in the vast majority of wagons entirely dependent upon the starting-point load, and, as has already been mentioned, it is not a unit which can be so effectively controlled by an individual railway as the originating average load. It is, however, a unit used largely and with great advantage for the purpose of statistical comparisons when measuring operating performances one period compared with another. Both figures are published by the Ministry of Transport in their monthly issue of railway statistics.

I think it would now be well to explain the method of ascertaining these average loads. For the purpose of ascertaining the average load of wagons at starting point each station governing a loading point is required to keep a daily record which will show the number of wagons loaded and the weight of the contents in each separately. The total number of wagons loaded is divided into the total weight loaded, this giving the average load for each day. The daily results are carefully examined by the goods agent, or on his behalf, and any defect discerned is made the subject of prompt inquiry.

To arrive at the average load hauled, the ton miles should be divided by the loaded wagon miles, which is the process adopted by the Ministry of Transport for arriving at their published figures showing the average load carried in the loaded wagons run over the railways in Great Britain. It will be appreciated that this statistic cannot be so promptly produced as the starting-point average load unit, as ton miles and wagon miles cannot be compiled until some time after the event. It is not therefore a daily statistic, but is usually compiled in four-weekly or calendar monthly periods.

The tabulation of these results period by period is useful. At station "A" its average load despatched in one period can be compared with corresponding periods in previous years, as well as period by period for each year. More than that, station "A" can be looked at in conjunction with stations "B," "C," "D," or any other station where comparison would or might be of value, and these comparisons in the hands of experts soon become suggestive and illuminating.

Where stations of similar circumstances as regards traffic commodities dealt with are found to vary greatly in regard to their loads, an inquiry will at once be made by the superintendent, and when evidence is collected together which shows clearly the reasons why certain stations are capable of regularly getting good loads where other stations fail, probably a meeting of officers concerned will be held to exchange notes, and such meetings are sure to result in the less expert persons gaining various "wrinkles" and picking up suggestions for improvement in their own work which will make them more skilful thereafter.

The circumstances of traffic must be very similar when comparisons of this kind are being made, or else the statements will be used for wrong purposes and much valuable time will be wasted. For instance, one station or group of stations show an average load per wagon despatched of 8·95 tons, whilst another station or group of stations shows an average of 3·23 tons. Unless and until the facts are known, namely, that at the smaller load stations the character of the traffic includes flour, manure, and fruit, whilst at the other roadstone, ores, and clay are the main staple commodity, the comparisons are of little value. On the other hand, at a general tranship shed where two or three thousand wagons of average traffic in sundry parcels are being dealt with, if it be found that the average at one station were regularly widely different from another similarly circumstanced, or the comparisons were to show marked fluctuations, an inquiry as to the reasons affecting the figures would be sure to lead to useful consideration.

Mossop gives figures [1] to show what a great variation there may be in the loads of *the same commodity* at different stations, thus :—

Sawn timber	varies from	3·30 to 4·25	tons
Flour	,, ,,	3·96 to 5·78	,,
Paper	,, ,,	3·48 to 5·95	,,
Cattle cake	,, ,,	2·03 to 4·64	,,

[1] These figures are given as actual records by Mossop (*Railway Operating Statistics*, p. 25).

We may give some figures as to what constitutes a good wagon load of various traffics. It must be understood that a 10- or 12-ton wagon, being a wagon for general use, may be used for fruit, feathers or ores, and that it is only when it has the heavy traffic such as ores that it can get the maximum load it was built for, so that very often, even when loaded to its full *cubical* capacity, a full load may fall short of its plated capacity.

The following figures have been prepared by one of the railway companies to show the maximum load which can be packed into a 10- or 12-ton wagon of different kinds of traffic: they are very useful as indicating how traffic varies in weight:—

Commodity.	Weight of Load when Wagon is Full.	
	10-Ton Open Wagon.	12-Ton Covered Wagon.
	T. C.	T. C.
Ale in barrels	4 4	6 3
Ale empties	0 16	2 10
Bacon in cases	9 0	—
Barytes	10 0	—
Linseed cake	8 0	12 0
Carrots (loose)	5 15	8 0
Cement, whiting, clay, fireclay ..	10 0	12 0
Eggs in boxes	3 0	6 0
Beans	10 0	12 0
Malt	6 0	11 5
Grease and tallow	5 0	12 0
Hay (press packed)	2 0	—
Iron and steel, Class "C"	10 0	—
Lead	10 0	12 0
Manure (town and stable)	9 0	—
Millboards	6 0	12 0
Onions	6 0	10 10
Oranges	6 0	12 0
Paper	7 6	—
Sanitary tubes	4 0	—
Slag wool	2 10	4 0
Sugar in bags	10 0	12 0
Wood in bags	3 15	—

Capacity of Wagons.—The cubical and carrying capacity of wagons has a very important bearing on the average of the actual load carried, and whilst the question of capacity is more fully dealt with in the chapter on "Wagons and Tares," it may be well here to give the facts in regard to the relative carrying capacities in the three countries, U.S.A., England, and Germany.

In America there are 2,325,647 cars of all kinds, and these included (1914 record) no less than 56,006 wagons of an average capacity of 56 tons ; 3,485 wagons of 70 tons capacity ; 1 car of 110, and 3 of 142 tons capacity. The average capacity of the 2,325,000 wagons was (1914) about 37½ tons. These figures I took out before the war ; now the number of wagons is distinctly less, but the average capacity is about 42 tons. In Germany the figures for 1910 show that there were 171,937 covered wagons and 394,003 open wagons ; and these 566,000 wagons had an average capacity of 13·68 tons.[1]

As regards Great Britain, the only figures we have available are those of the North Eastern Railway, which are given by Mossop in *Railway Operating Statistics* (from 1901 to 1911). By the courtesy of the company I am able to continue the figures for the more recent years. It is generally understood that this company, which is perhaps fortunately situated, has been able to do more than others in encouraging the use of large capacity wagons upon its system. The figures may be taken as indicating steady growth in England and exhibiting the same tendency towards larger operating units which we have shown is so conspicuous on the other side of the Atlantic.

The following are the figures :—

AVERAGE CARRYING CAPACITIES OF N.E.R. WAGON STOCK.

Year.	Goods Wagons.	Mineral Wagons.	Year.	Goods Wagons.	Mineral Wagons.
1901	8·06	10·06	1910	9·21	12·76
1902	8·08	10·14	1911	9·36	12·83
1903	8·05	10·36	1912	9·70	13·00
1904	8·15	10·88	1913	9·87	13·02
1905	8·54	11·44	*	*	*
1906	8·74	11·66	1919	10·50	13·41
1907	8·84	12·03	1920	10·69	13·45
1908	9·03	12·29	1921	10·87	14·00
1909	9·10	12·61			

[1] In 1915 this figure had been further increased to 14·7 ; since then figures are not obtainable.

In the standard statistical information which railway companies have to publish under statutory requirements (Act of 1911) provision is made for information as to vehicles owned by each railway company—(1) of over 20 tons capacity; (2) over 12 tons and up to 20 tons; (3) over 8 tons and up to 12 tons.

We may now consider the effect in practical financial saving of any improvement shown in these figures. Mossop plunges into the heart of the matter and puts the case in a very practical way when he says:—

> A railway which must move 1,000,000 tons in the busiest month in the year would require with an average load of 3 tons and a loaded journey every four days a stock of 47,619 wagons. If the load were 3½ tons on the average, a stock of 40,816 wagons would be required, or a reduction of 6,803 wagons.

This is a concrete enough saving, but it is only a first step in stating the total economy effected. Let us assume a railway company is able in the course of a few years to increase the average of its freight wagon load by 20 per cent. (the North Eastern Railway between 1904 and 1920 increased from 5·11 to 6·16 tons), and let us consider in detail the sort and extent of economy that would result.

Firstly as regards wagon maintenance: if the average load per wagon is increased by 20 per cent., the same stock of wagons will suffice to carry an increased traffic of 20 per cent., and the saving so represented will be large. Assuming it to be 20 per cent. for the whole country, it would represent an annual economy of about three-quarters of a million sterling on pre-war costs—more than double that under more recent circumstances. Secondly, the relief of congestion on the main lines, in the shunting yards, and at the terminals will also be considerable. Thirdly, a reduction in the number of train miles is bound to follow on a reduction of anything like 20 per cent. in the number of loaded wagons. There will probably not be the same percentage reduction in train miles as in wagon miles, but it should represent a very large saving in engine power. In mineral working, for instance, if a colliery has an output of 3,000 tons per day, and the average wagon load is increased from 10 to 12 tons, the train load will be increased in somewhat similar ratio, and the number of trains to carry the daily output will be reduced in ratio not far, if at all, short of the increase in the wagon load. Take the number of goods train miles run by the L. & N.W. Company in 1913 as 17,500,000 ; if only one-half the ratio of reduction, i.e. 10 per cent., were effected as in the number of wagons used, there would be a saving of a million and three quarters goods train miles, representing not less than £100,000 per annum. Fourthly, the capacity of the railway systems would be enlarged by having fewer trains and fewer wagons to deal with : this is an unmeasurable quantity. But if anything like the above figures of saving could be realised, the improvement in economy would be enormous ; and it must be remembered that we are only speaking of the one question of the improved loading of wagons.

The question of actually larger wagons or larger engines and bigger trains is a further factor quite outside what we are dealing with in connection with the loads of wagons. The question of improved tares of wagons is dealt with in Chapter IX, and therefore it is unnecessary at present to deal with that aspect of the matter.

We cannot perhaps better conclude this chapter than by emphasising the importance of the question of improvement in wagon loading, and we would recapitulate in summary form the directions in which in the future we may look for an increase in the loads conveyed in our British stock of goods wagons.

1. Improved loading of individual wagons at all goods stations.
2. Improved and better organised system of transhipping co-ordinated as between all railway companies.
3. Gradual improvement in size and capacity of wagons in general use.
4. More economical ratio of tare to contents load of wagons.

CHAPTER VII

LOADERS AND LOADING

We have in the preceding chapter dwelt at some length with the question of an average or normal wagon load, and emphasised the great variation according to the kinds of traffic with which we may for the time being be dealing. Not only do the loads differ very greatly according to the particular traffic, but the wagons and their capacities are themselves also a very variable factor, varying according to the classes of commodities for which provision has to be made, or the differing views held by the railway companies in regard to their construction.

We have said little so far as to the human or personal factor and its bearing on the load question, but it is a very important factor. One has only to watch with a little continuity a wagon loader employed at a large goods station, and see the miscellaneous character of the traffic he is dealing with, in order to realise that the man who loads needs to be an expert. Straw hats, iron bars, earthenware in crates, cauliflowers, bags of yeast, soft fruit—hard and soft goods and commodities of all shapes and sizes. When an untrained recruit stands before a miscellaneous assortment comprising articles of the kind above mentioned and many more and has to " stow " them into a wagon for conveyance we can imagine something of his chagrin or of his difficulty in knowing where to begin. The trained loader knows that with the starting and often sudden stopping of the train any heavy articles will have a tendency to move backwards or forwards in the wagon by virtue of their inherent momentum, and that such movement may have an uncomfortable and very prejudicial effect upon any softer goods immediately behind or in front; that apart from starting and stopping, the continuous oscillation and jolting of the train also causes much shifting movement within the van or wagon ; and that chafing and breakage in transit is one of the main causes of damage and claims. It is the loader's business to learn how to load and stow goods in such a manner as to result in a minimum of damage from the causes named. This is one of the main features to which the loader must have regard, apart altogether from the question of how to get the maximum quantity of goods loaded in a minimum of room.

A good loader, therefore, must of necessity be a man of experience. Such a man, whether his work be amongst the miscellaneous assortment of a town goods warehouse or in the timber yard at Hull or Hartlepool, or at a cotton warehouse at Liverpool, in the fruit and vegetable areas of Hampshire or Cambridge, may easily be able to secure in his wagon a load of 40 or 50 per cent. more goods than the inexperienced novice. In certain districts and places where special traffics are dealt with, the loader will be further differentiated, as for instance the loader of timber, cotton, or fruit, as above referred to. Timber loading is a special art, needing much skill with rough timber in an unsawn condition, consisting of tree trunks of varying sizes and shapes and lengths up to 100 feet or more. Timber loaders generally work in gangs, with a chief or loading man, and the gang will have to be prepared to move to this or that rural station wherever it may be when "rough" or "round" timber needs to be dispatched. It is a skilled business to secure half a dozen unwieldy and unshapely tree trunks on to a set of trucks in such a manner as will allow of longitudinal and lateral play in stopping and starting and rounding curves during transit, so that they will remain firm and travel steadily on the wagons during a long journey, surviving without accident through dislodgement the often continuous jogging and jolting of the wagon and load during conveyance.

Some of the railway companies have issued careful loading regulations for the guidance of their men whose duty it is to load wagons : these regulations are usually accompanied by diagrams and illustrations setting out the principal points which the loader must be careful to observe, and generally aimed at instructing the men how they may most effectively secure good loads.

At this point we may refer to the wages of the men. In the pre-war days the relationship between the grades of porter, loader, and checker is very well represented by the respective wages which at typical busy stations were as follows: porters, 21s., 22s., or 23s. per week (graded probably over three years); loaders or stowers, 24s., 25s. (first and second or subsequent years' service in grade); checkers, 26s., 27s. 6d., 30s., 32s. 6d., according to rank and character of station. The effect of war has been to raise all these wages up to a much higher level, and the standard rates of porters vary from 40s. to 44s. per week, and for checkers from 47s. to 54s. per week, although at the present time many of the men are receiving considerably more than these rates per week at stations in the large industrial areas (leaving London out of account where the figures are higher still). These higher figures represent the range of the goods warehousemen or station staff below the rank of foremen, i.e. from porter to head checker. This subject will come up for consideration again when we deal with the organisation of a goods station; meantime it should be here pointed out that the distinction between the goods porter and loader would appear to be the commencing line of demarcation between the unskilled labourer and skilled artisan in so far as railway goods work is concerned, if such distinction is to be preserved in the circumstances of the future railway world. The loader's work is part of the transport machine: his service is in connection with the movement of wagons, whilst the porter's service of barrowing is unskilled.

The view will doubtless be held by some that the drawing of any exact line between the work or service of a loader and a checker, or on the other hand of a goods porter and loader, is in practice impossible; but the considerations above set out make it clear wherein the difference in theory and in definition exists. In practice it is always an advantage that one grade should know something of the point of view and responsibility of the grades with whom he has to work in co-operation; the porter or barrowman should always be pleased if permitted or requested to do the work of a loader in abnormal circumstances (for it trains him for more extended responsibility in the future), and the loader will find it of real help to know as much as he can learn of the duties of the checker above him : it will make his own work both more agreeable and more effective. More than that, the question of loyal and earnest co-operation between grades such as the three just now named, whose work is so closely bound together, is a factor than which throughout the whole of the goods station working there is none more important. The function of the foreman in maintaining and stimulating this close and keen co-operation, a function not always recognised as it should be, is dealt with in Chapter X.

As this chapter is dealing with the human factor and its influence upon the development of the load, we ought further to emphasise the importance of co-operation : it comes in at almost every turn in the organisation of a great railway—or indeed of any other industrial system.

One might almost say that the amount of supervision (on the part of a foreman at any rate) required bears a relation in inverse proportion to the degree of co-operation between those over whom he is placed in authority. And not only is co-operation a principal asset within the goods station itself, but it is almost equally important it should obtain between the yard staff (shunters, etc.) outside and the staff working within the goods station shed ; for the obtaining and "setting" of suitable wagons at the benches, and the drawing out of stock as soon as loaded, rests with the shunting staff outside. The assistant yard master or the yard foreman must therefore be in very close touch to secure that the wagon working is carried out effectively, and that the needs of the goods station are understood by the staff working in the marshalling yard outside.

As soon as the loading staff becomes really keen to secure a constantly improving average load figure at the particular station where they are employed, they will find that in the selection of wagons for bench working there is room for the display of no little ingenuity on the part of the yard master if he is considering the interests of the station loaders and knows the class of wagon which they favour for getting good loading results. This opportunity of selection, moreover, has considerably extended since the arrangement was made by the companies for all ordinary goods wagons to be pooled.

The yard master who in many cases will have both the marshalling yard or shunting sidings and the goods station itself under his supervision is able—now that the pooling of wagons is in operation—to select indiscriminately from the empty wagons in his sidings the number of wagons (say 60 or whatever be the quota) asked for by the goods station agent or foreman. In pre-pooling days the yard foreman would be limited to his own company's wagons only, and would be under the necessity of sending all the "foreign" wagons back to their separate systems, and communicate by telegram or the quickest available means with other stations, or the central wagon office, urging his requirement in the way of empty wagons. But we shall describe in greater detail in the next chapter the arrangement for the pooling or common user of wagons.

We have in this chapter dealt with the position of the goods station loader in relation to the porter and checker because the duties are to some extent interchangeable. At the smaller stations a goods porter perforce does the whole of the work which at larger stations is allotted to three different grades. We have in this goods station work a very good illustration of how the principle of division of labour works in practice. As the aggregation of traffic to be dealt with at large stations becomes a greater factor, the grades of staff become differentiated, as will be described fully in Chapter X.

It is a not uncommon practice at British goods stations where many loaders are at work to pay the men on a system of bonus in addition to the standard time wages. Under this system a loader is paid an additional wage or bonus for every additional ton that he loads per day, or per week, as the case may be. This system, although it has undoubtedly given a fillip to expeditious loading, is not one which obtains favour by the men at large, and has undoubtedly some disadvantages. The whole subject of loading at goods stations is further dealt with in the chapter upon the "Organisation of a Goods Station."

CHAPTER VIII

COMMON USER OF GOODS WAGONS

THE question of the use of railway-owned wagons in common by all railway companies, ignoring individual company ownership, and so allowing each company to use the stock of another company as it would its own, has so very direct a bearing upon the whole question of the effective utilisation of the wagon stock of the country or of any individual railway company that it is necessary to set out the facts of the present position, and to describe briefly the stages which have led up to it.

We would first set out shortly in historic sequence the stages by which the railway companies have gradually arrived at a fairly complete arrangement for, shall I say, indiscriminate user of each other's wagons, or what is generally termed "common user." The privately-owned wagons (650,000 out of a total British stock of about 1,400,000) still remain, of course, outside the arrangement, as well as certain types of railway owned wagons, such as stock constructed for specific requirements of traffic originating on an individual company's system, e.g. banana vans, refrigerator cars, trollies, etc.

Towards the end of the year 1915, the Great Eastern, Great Northern, and Great Central Railway Companies, who had for some years been working under an agreement for the pooling of their resources wherever practicable, agreed amongst themselves upon an arrangement under which they recognised the common user of one another's wagons as though they were all under the same ownership ; this group or trio of companies was known as the Eastern Group, and in the spring of the next year (1916) five other large companies, namely the G.W., L. & N.W., Midland, L. & Y., and

N.E. agreed upon a similar arrangement and formed a separate group amongst themselves. So things went on for some time under two separate groups, each of which were recognising a common stock of wagons throughout the group. But meantime the Government had been taking some initiative to get all the railway companies *and the private owners of railway wagons* to pool their stock throughout the country, and meeting after meeting took place between the Government and the wagon owners.

It was estimated that of the private owners' wagons, 500,000 were mineral wagons, and many of these colliery wagons were built specially to accommodate the circumstances of a particular colliery yard, and they would be found quite unsuited to another colliery. The description of brake fitted to the wagon and the variation of doors (side, bottom, or end)—all these features needed to be carefully considered in relation not only to the colliery sidings but also to the cranes and discharging apparatus at the docks and other receiving points to which these private wagons were habitually worked. After many meetings and protracted negotiations, the Board of Trade was perforce driven to admit that a general all-round user of railway and private owned wagons was impracticable, not only because many types of wagon would still have to be kept for use in particular localities, which was an important factor, but also from the difficulty of financial adjustment.

But the Minister of Transport showed a determination to pursue this matter further, and in the Ministry of Transport Bill (1919) he took power to take over on certain terms the whole of the privately owned traders' wagons; and on the first reading of the bill the minister announced that this was one of the first reforms he intended to accomplish when the bill passed into law. This it did in August 1919, but so far the difficulties in the way of the purchase of traders' wagons by the government have not been overcome, and they remain as yet private property.

Whilst the Board of Trade was busy with this negotiation, the Lancashire and Yorkshire Railway Company had actually got into operation a plan agreed upon with some of the colliery owners on their line under which, in order to obviate the back-working of so many empty colliery wagons from port to colliery, any wagon after being discharged at the port of Liverpool might be loaded up with a load of goods in the direction of its normal home journey. The arrangement seems simple and reasonable enough, but it was not agreed upon except after much protest from the wagon owners, who asseverated it was bound to mean serious detention of their colliery stock.

But practice showed that the reverse of this predicted detention actually resulted, that in fact the wagons when loaded with goods found their way home faster than they used to do as "empties"; for as empties they could only come forward when engine power was available; as loaded wagons they were worked forward by first available train, taking precedence over empty wagon working. So often it is the unexpected that happens. And this practical example of utilisation of empty mineral wagons became a very useful precedent as news of the success of the experiment gradually permeated the ranks of the practical railwaymen on other systems.

As might have been expected, the two groups of railway systems known as "The Three Greats" and "The Five Companies" had not been working independently for many months before conferences took place between them and other railway companies, some of whom had been considering an arrangement between themselves. One result of these conferences was that in June 1916 the Scottish companies brought a common user scheme into operation similar to that of "The Fives" group. Subsequent to this discussions ensued with the object of ascertaining whether it would not be possible to amalgamate forces further and have one general common user of wagon stock. The outcome of these discussions was that as from the beginning of 1917 all the principal companies of England, Scotland, and Wales agreed to recognise as a "common user" wagon all their ordinary "open" as distinguished from covered or box wagons which conformed to certain dimensional specifications: these are set out in the following extract from the *Board of Trade Journal* wherein the arrangement was publicly announced:—

The Railway Companies' Wagons.

Curiously enough, it proved, after careful investigation, not much more feasible to pool all railway-owned wagons than it had been to pool the private wagons. The chief obstacles were the absence of standardisation in the construction of the various companies' wagons, and the fact that various classes of wagons were necessarily kept for certain classes of goods. One cannot, for example, load coal into a covered cattle truck. Many wagons, too, had been built to suit the discharging appliances at certain ports or works, and were quite unsuited for other ports or works where the equipment was wholly different. These divergencies between the types and use of wagons limited the possibility of a common user for all of them. But although there could be no means devised to utilise all wagons for all purposes, steps were taken successfully to group definite classes of wagons together and to make use of them by the railway companies as joint equipment. Combinations for a common user of specified types of wagons were made by groups of railway companies, and on January 2, 1917, the Railway Executive Committee brought into operation a common user, subject to certain exceptions, by all companies of ordinary open wagons, with sides of three or more planks, and with doors on both sides the full height of the wagon. This meant that some 300,000 wagons of a generally useful type, belonging to the controlled companies of Great Britain, would become available for use in any direction upon all the companies' lines. A committee of railway representatives was set up to "equate" the wagons as between one company and another, and to ensure that they were distributed to the needs of all. To this extent the railway-owned wagons were pooled for general service.

All the wagons which conformed to the standard specified in the paragraph quoted above came thenceforward to be free to move about over all the railways where they might be needed, just as though they were at home on their own line.

There was to be no charge for use of one company's wagon by another railway. As regards all wagons not coming under the standard dimensions indicated, they were to go on as before as separately owned wagons, requiring to be sent back home empty as soon as liberated.

The necessary machinery of organisation had to be set up to give effect to these arrangements, and this involved the following :—

1. At every junction a record was taken of common user wagons passing on to or coming off each separate system.

2. At the end of each week the balance of wagons in favour of or against each company to be adjusted by a prompt return of any excess of wagons obtained by an individual company.

3. A weekly meeting of representatives of all companies to constitute a central Wagon Control committee, and to give effect to all the necessary adjustments as between companies.

This common user of wagons, even though confined to a section of the general wagon stock, gave very great relief and secured a vast economy in wagon stock. One of the most significant ways in which this economy has shown itself is in the reduced proportion of empty wagon mileage out of the total wagon mileage incurred in the country. After a year's experience it was generally stated to have effected a reduction in the mileage of empty wagon running which had been 33 per cent. of the total to 16 per cent., and the practical railwaymen who tasted of the economies and improvements effected very soon began to advocate that the pooling arrangement should extend to other classes of stock.

The change herein indicated was not given effect to without many hindrances and difficulties : it is because of this we have set out fully the story of the adoption of the change. A railway wagon builder naturally likes to repair his own stock, and in case of breakdown of a wagon in a distant part of England under the system which calls a wagon "at home" anywhere, and it is placed in a break-down, not-to-go, or hospital siding, with (say) a broken spring, it finds itself really no more "at home" than is a fish out of water. But how is it to be repaired? The journals or brake fittings, springs or oil-boxes may be of a very different type from those generally in use on the lines of the company on whose system it has broken down. There is always some way out of these temporary difficulties, and under these circumstances special arrangements were made for the conveyance by passenger train of the necessary parts or fittings from the original wagon builders to the shops of the railway company on whose line the breakdown occurred, and subsequently for parts usually wanted in the repair of other companies' wagons to be exchanged and held in stock at certain centres so as to minimise passenger train conveyance of the material. These arrangements work well and obviate the incurring of hundreds of wagon miles which would be involved if the wagon had to be returned to the parent company. One has only to look inside one of our large despatching goods warehouses at the time of day when the warehouse is being "set" with wagons for the outward despatch of its traffic to see how great is the additional facility accruing from the ability of the agent or yard master to lay hold of any company's wagon in the yard and set it for its load irrespective of destination, instead of carefully providing an L. & Y. wagon for L. & Y. stations, a G.W. wagon for the G.W. system, a Cambrian wagon for Wales, and so on.

The question that has been referred to as a difficulty in regard to repairing of wagons when away from home may yet turn out to be something of a blessing in disguise, for it must of necessity result in a concentration of attention upon the importance of further standardisation amongst British railway wagon builders. The more that interchange and common user of stock becomes prevalent in England, the greater will the need of standardisation be felt, and the more there is a combination (instead of competition) in engineering ability and skill in the construction of the best designs of wagon stock, the less difficulty should there be in point of fact in determining the best practical standards. Any consideration of the varying types of wagons in operation to-day such as we have—only shortly and summarily—ventured to embark upon in Chapter IX on "Wagons and Tares" must emphasise the urgent importance of this question.

A good deal could be said of the advantages which have been derived from the common user of stock in the country. I do not, however, propose to dwell upon these, but will content myself by mentioning some of the principal of them :—

1. Greater availability of stock.
2. Saving in empty wagon haulage.
3. Relief at exchange points, many of which were experiencing congestion.
4. Reduction in shunting and economy in engine power.
5. Less wagon standage accommodation required in goods yards, private sidings, docks, etc.

It is interesting to learn how Germany has been busy with this same question, and has been proceeding on very similar lines to those we have adopted since 1915, although she anticipated us in her consideration of the question and her definite action upon it. Germany too is increasing the size of her wagons, steadily substituting a capacity of 15 or 20 tons for 10 tons as she rebuilds her stock; indeed, a wagon marked with a capacity of less than 15 tons in Germany to-day is comparatively a *rara avis.*

In order to secure the maximum advantage in the use of her wagon stock, the federal railway authority in Germany called into being a committee of representatives under the name of the German States Railway wagon union, whose function was that of securing the common user of wagons throughout the German empire from Basel to Memel, so that each administration might make use of the wagons belonging to adjoining administrations as if they were its own, and all these arrangements are adjusted from a central office in Berlin. The results in the case of Germany are pronounced to be the avoidance of a large amount of empty wagon haulage, a general improvement in circulation, and much simplification in distribution—all being summed up in a reduced cost falling upon sender, consignee, and railway company.

In passing we may give the following facts as to the railway wagon stock of Germany: There were at the end of 1915 a stock of 725,071 wagons in Germany, with a capacity of 10,699,000 tons, giving an average wagon capacity of 14·7 tons. Of the total wagons named, 496,503 wagons, or 68 per cent., were open at the top; 228,568 wagons or 32 per cent., were of the covered or "box" type; and nearly the whole of these are at the general disposal of the central office of the Railway Wagon Union in Berlin.

In view of recent happenings in the land of Germany it may be of interest to give the following full particulars in regard to the years from 1906 to 1915 as to the capacity of the wagon stock of that country. The figures are as follows:—

GOODS WAGONS IN GERMANY: NUMBER AND CAPACITY.

Weight Capacity in Tons (Kilometric).

Year.	No. of Wagons.	Aggregate.	Per Wagon.
1906	467,064	6,182,000	13·3
1907	497,923	6,683,000	13·4
1908	521,746	7,098,000	13·6
1909	542,253	7,473,000	13·8
1910	565,940	7,890,000	13·9
1911	596,763	8,422,000	14·1
1912	627,403	9,005,000	14·4
1913	667,048	9,683,000	14·5
1914	696,488	10,231,000	14·7
1915	725,071	10,699,000	14·7

In the matter of continuous brakes in Germany the railway authorities have apparently made up their minds as to continuous brakes upon their goods wagons. Before the war a very large number of wagons in Prussia had been equipped with such brakes, but progress in regard to further equipment has since the war been arrested, pending a decision as to the particular type of brake to be adopted.

This principle of central control of which we have made mention as operating throughout the federal system of German states is one of such importance that we must devote a little more attention to the position before we leave this subject. Things have been moving very rapidly in Germany in recent years, and since the revolution of November 1918 there has been much development in the direction of unity. The different state organisations (or *direktionen*) of railways have become amalgamated into one centralised national system of railways (Reichsbahn), controlled from Berlin under the headship of a Minister of Transport, and all the separate state ownerships of rolling stock have disappeared. The wagons are now all Reichsbahn wagons, and the central control of various state ownerships has now become a control office for the economical distribution of one united national stock.

The Wagon Control Office is an essential piece of machinery with every large stock-owning railway company, if it is to use its wagon stock with advantage and economy. Picture for a moment if you can the daily position of any railway company with, say, 500 stations or loading and discharging points, including perhaps twenty large manufacturing towns and half a dozen important exporting docks. At the large dock systems (Liverpool, Southampton, Glasgow, etc.) empty wagons are in constant demand to load up the import traffic which is ordinarily in excess of the export. There are other docks, however, where goods are sent out of the country in greater quantity than they are imported. At such places there may be each day hundreds of railway wagons on hand empty, having discharged their contents into ships; there are the score of large producing towns at various points on the system, each wanting a good supply of empties, and at the four or five hundred wayside stations many have a surplus of wagons, whilst others have a considerable shortage of the stock they require for the loading up of goods they have ready for despatch.

The business of the Wagon Control Office is to visualise daily (or two or three times per day) the needs, in the matter of wagons, of all the loading points of the system, to gain a knowledge of the locus of all the empty wagons upon the line; and by bringing these two factors together, to proceed to distribute the stock as to secure the utmost economy in its use.

In times of slack trade it may be that two or three thousand wagons will have to be taken out of circulation and stored or laid up in some spare unused sidings; occasionally it will be found the available stock is 5, 10, or 15 per cent. short of the demands for it, and then the supply of available units will have to be distributed to applying stations in quantities short of their tabulated needs in as impartial a manner as is possible.

To enable the Wagon Control Office to make the necessary adjustments and allocations, very accurate information must necessarily be collected. This will include :—

1. A return from every station and loading point of all the empty wagons it has on hand at the conclusion of each day.
2. The number of loaded wagons received at and despatched from every station day by day.
3. The additional wagons each station requires for the next day's loading, or the surplus it has to spare.
4. Special returns of the number of empty wagons standing at 6.0 p.m. or other stated period in the empty wagon siding at the large dock centres and at the important marshalling yards.
5. Empty wagons coming on to the railway system from foreign junctions, or from other places where empties are "made,"—as e.g. at a seaport where the export traffic is greater than the import.

The question of wagon control as part of the whole question of the centralised technical control of railway and train working is too large to be dealt with in any detail in this chapter, and this outline of what is meant by centralised wagon control must suffice for present purposes. A central wagon control office has come to be recognised as a *sine qua non* in any well organised railway system.

The taking of an occasional sample or test census of wagon loads, as adopted by some companies, is also a very useful and practical method of assisting supervision. This is given effect to by a request from headquarters for a return for a week selected at probably three or four different seasons of the year, giving information from all the stations on the system as to the average loads of all wagons despatched from each station classified under the headings of certain groups of traffic, thus :—

........STATION, W.E., 21/4/1918.

Description of Traffic.	No. of wagons.	Total weight.	Average load per wagon.
		T. C.	T. C.
Coal and coke ..	24,652	248,281 10	10 1
Other minerals ..	3,760	37,794 5	10 1
General merchandise	6,794	31,871 18	4 14
Company's stores ..	2,060	23,247 12	11 6
Station trucks ..	113	261 10	2 6
Total : all wagons	41,236	341,456 15	8 6

If this return is followed up year after year for the same period of the year by similar sample returns, a useful record of progress (or the reverse) will be established ; and where the system of daily returns for the Central Wagon Control Office has been established, the additional labour in taking out sample returns of this kind will probably be greatly reduced.

CHAPTER IX

WAGONS AND TARES

No student of railway economics can fail to become aware as soon as he turns his attention to the wagon question in Great Britain of the importance of the question of standardisation of wagon types, and of some of the advantages that would accrue if there were some attempt at the adoption of a certain number of standard wagon types on the part of the united companies to suit the different conditions of traffic that require transport.

The comparatively recent decision of the English, Scotch, and Welsh railway companies to use the bulk of the railway-owned wagons in common has drawn the attention of the "practical man" to the advantage to be derived from this. Apart from the mere student, both the rank and file and many of the railway officers are convinced that rigorous steps ought to be taken as soon as possible to secure a very wide movement towards a standardisation of railway wagons. The perhaps natural bias on the part of many officers and servants alike in favour of the wagon they have been used to on their own system whilst it remained a separate and competing system is no doubt the main factor in the way of any speedy alteration.

It needs only a glance at the table set out on page 20 to realise the great variety of wagons that exist, but apart from this evidence on paper the fact is the more pronounced, and indeed it becomes impressive, if one looks critically or even casually at any haphazard collection of wagons standing in a siding or running on a train, notwithstanding the requirement that the vehicles must be constructed within standard specifications in all their parts.

It is not the tare weights only that differ: the principal

dimensions, length, height of sides, description of wheels, buffers, grease or oil boxes, springs—indeed every part has almost infinite variations according to the taste, ideas, or caprice of the builder or the traffic operator who has to manipulate the wagon movements.

We do not presume in any dogmatic manner to prescribe what are the best types of wagons to suit the conditions of all British railway systems, but simply to point out the facts making for or against standardisation, and draw attention to certain of the principal types that are now in general use in the country. We may say at the outset that, apart from the standard types specifically referred to, there must of necessity be on every company's line a certain number of wagons of exceptional type which have been called into being to meet special circumstances and which would probably need to be retained for local user whatever general system of standardisation may be determined upon. Let nobody think that those who advocate some effort after standardisation have any expectation that every separate type of wagon in the country must hereafter be made to conform to a few predetermined standards settled in London which will apply as the only and invariable types of wagon which will be permitted.

The principal types of wagon of which practically all the larger companies have a certain number in stock to-day may be set out as follows :—

Ordinary open goods wagon.
Ordinary covered goods wagon (or box wagon).
10- or 12-ton mineral wagon.
20-ton mineral wagon.
Timber wagon.
Cattle wagon.

Even in regard to each of these types there is a difference not only in the component parts—axles, wheels, oil-boxes, brakes, etc.—but also in regard to leading dimensions. Nearly every company has its difference in standard parts.

In the illustration of a mixed train of 61 wagons on

Fig. 11.—Ordinary High-Sided Goods Wagon, N.E.R. 12 Tons Capacity.

page 20, if the actual wagons were examined, it would be found that hardly any two were built to a specific standard pattern : probably there may be 40 or 50 varieties of wagon.

But if we examine the load, there seems to be no very good reason why the whole train should not be made up of the six standards just named, if there were any determined and united disposition to secure standardisation. Perhaps this illustration affords as good an indication as can be desired as to what standardisation could accomplish.

Let us take the first four of the above types of wagon in order :—

1. *Ordinary Open or High-sided Goods Wagon.*—This is the most common type of goods wagon on the British railways. We give illustrations of two of these wagons—a Lancashire and Yorkshire and a North Eastern Railway wagon (Figs. 11 and 12). The principal dimensions are as follows :—

		N.E.	L. & Y.
Length over all, i.e. over buffers	ft.	20 0	23 0
Length over head-stocks	,,	17 0	20 0
Inside length of wagon	,,	16 7	19 7
Length of wheel-base	,,	9 6	10 6
Plated capacity	tons	12 0 0	12 0 0
Dimensions of journals (up to 15 tons) ..	ins.	9 × 4½	9 × 4¼
Tare weight of wagon	tons	6 9 0	6 9 0

We give the particulars of this wagon because it is the ordinary wagon which was first taken as the "common user" wagon.

2. *Covered-in or Box Wagon.*—There is a great variety of these covered wagons, but the standard which appears to have been evolved as the best and most serviceable is that represented by the two pictures given of the latest type of covered wagon on the L. & Y. and N.E.R. systems—see illustrations (Figs. 13 and 14).

Some companies in the construction of these wagons regularly adopt the practice of movable tops or ceilings—of the roller shutter type—so that when necessary for a crane to be used in loading heavy articles, the top can be rolled back.

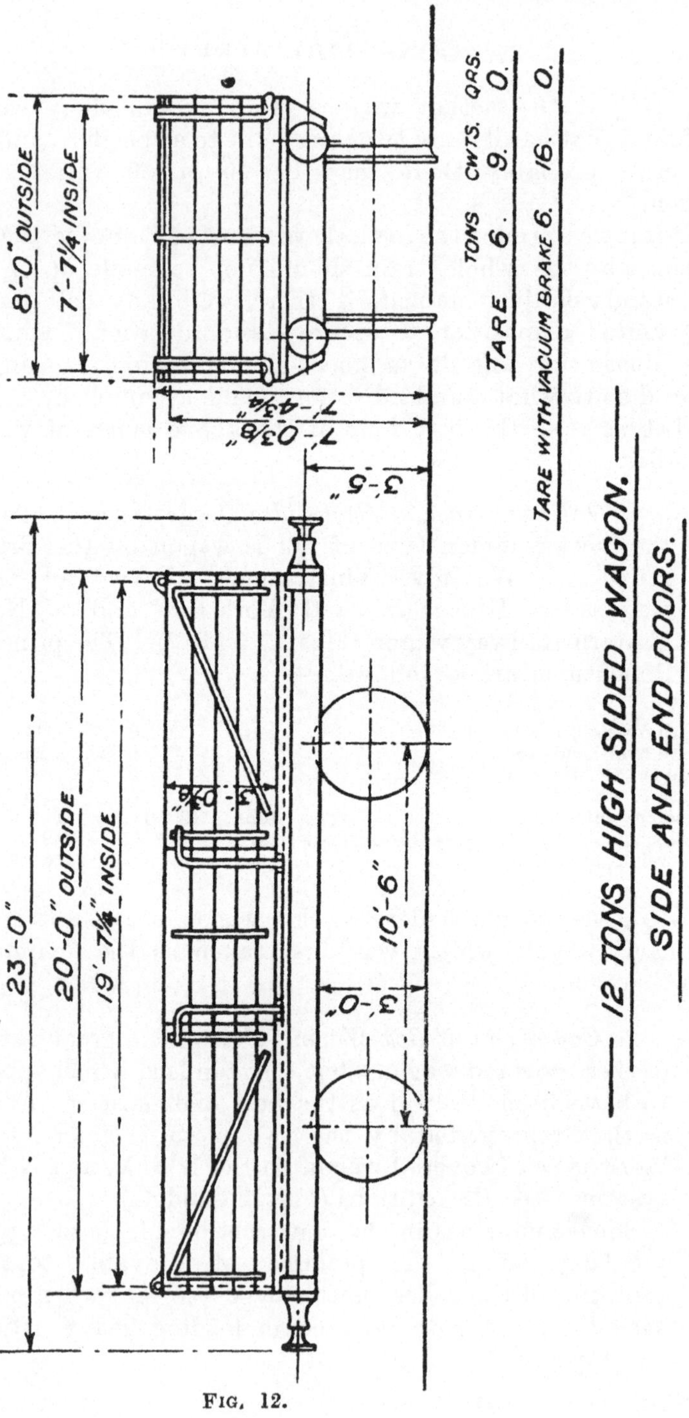
8'-0" OUTSIDE
7'-7¼ INSIDE
TONS CWTS. QRS.
TARE 6. 9. 0.
TARE WITH VACUUM BRAKE 6. 16. 0.
7'-4¾"
7'-0⅜"
3'-5"
12 TONS HIGH SIDED WAGON.
SIDE AND END DOORS.
23'-0"
20'-0" OUTSIDE
19'-7¼" INSIDE
3'-0⅜"
10'-6"
3'-0"

FIG. 12.

Fig. 13.—Covered-in or Box Wagon, N.E.R. 12 Tons Capacity.

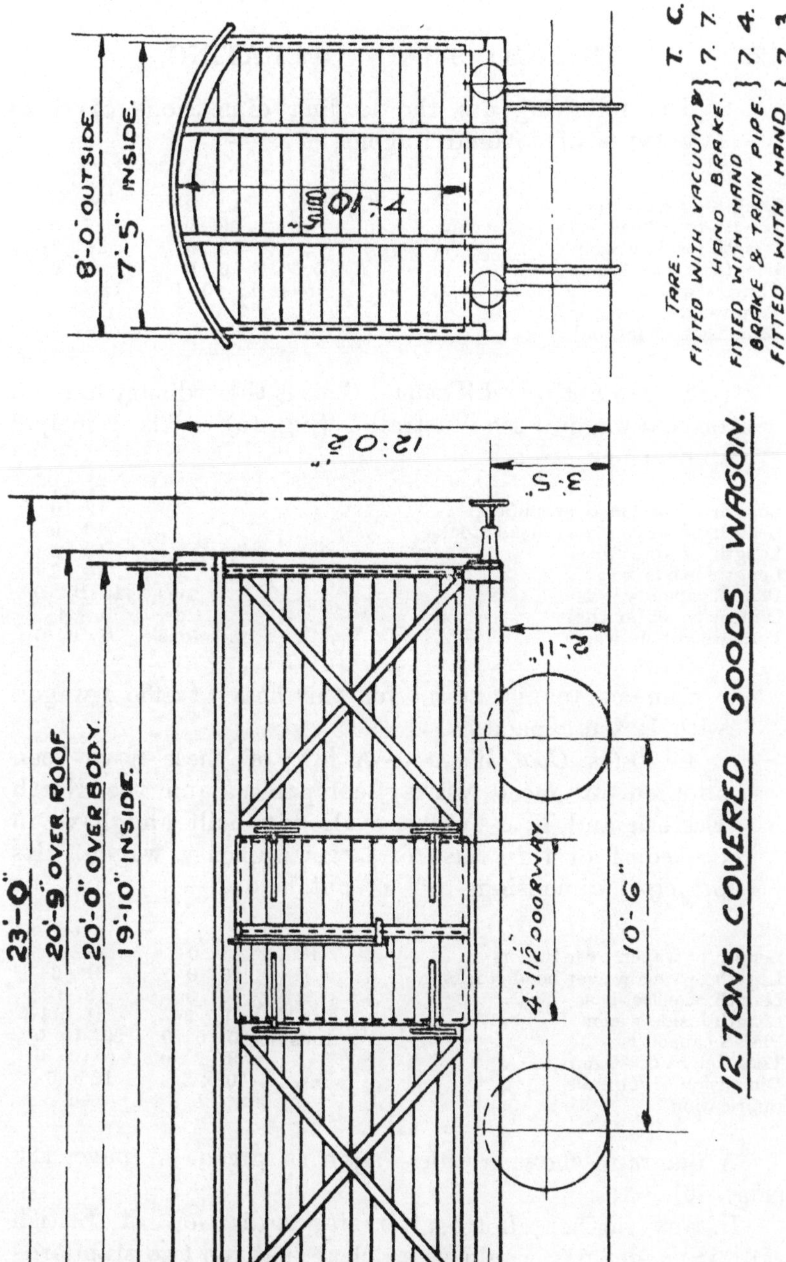
23'-0"
20'-9" OVER ROOF
20'-0" OVER BODY
19'-10" INSIDE
4'-11½" DOORWAY
10'-6"
3'-5"
12'-0½"
8'-0" OUTSIDE
7'-5" INSIDE
12 TONS COVERED GOODS WAGON.
TARE. T. C. Q
FITTED WITH VACUUM & HAND BRAKE. 7. 7. 2.
FITTED WITH HAND BRAKE & TRAIN PIPE. 7. 4. 0
FITTED WITH HAND BRAKE ONLY. 7. 3. 0.

Fig. 14.

The following are the leading dimensions of these two types of covered wagons, viz. :—

		L. & Y.	N.E.R.
Length over buffers	ft.	23 0	20 0
Length over head-stocks	,,	20 9	17 0
Length inside wagon	,,	19 10	16 3½
Length of wheel-base	,,	10 6	9 6
Plated capacity	tons	12 0 0	12 0 0
Tare weight of wagon	,,	7 7 2	6 18 0
Dimension of journals	ins.	9 × 4¼	9 or 9½ × 4¼

3. 10-*ton Mineral Wagon.*—This is the ordinary mineral or coal wagon—see illustration (Fig. 15). The principal dimensions are :—

		Ft. in.
Length of wagon over buffers		19 10
Length of wagon over head-stocks		16 6
Length of wheel-base		10 6
Length inside wagon		16 2
Plated capacity	tons	10 10 0
Dimension of journals	ins.	9 × 4¼
Tare weight of wagon	tons	6 9 0

Some companies adopt for this heavy traffic a wagon with 12 ton capacity.

4. 20-*ton Coal Wagon.*—A few of these have been adopted by most railway companies, and the North Eastern and L. & Y. have already built and have in use some of this class of larger capacity wagon. Its principal dimensions are set out below :—

		N.E.R.	L. & Y.
Length of wagon over buffers	ft.	23 0	24 6
Length of wagon over head-stocks ..	,,	20 0	21 6
Length of wheel-base	,,	10 6	12 0
Length inside wagon	,,	19 7	21 1¼
Plated capacity	tons	20 0 0	20 0 0
Tare weight of wagon	,,	8 2 0	9 10 0
Dimension of journals	ins.	10 × 5	10 × 5
Lubrication		Oil	Oil

A diagram showing this wagon is given on page 123 (Fig. 16).

In any further efforts after standardisation of British railway wagons it would seem clear that the two standards of open and covered goods wagon should be continued, and as many as possible of the parts that go to make up these types should be standardised for construction and repair

Fig. 15.—Coal Wagon, N.E.R. 10½ Tons Capacity.

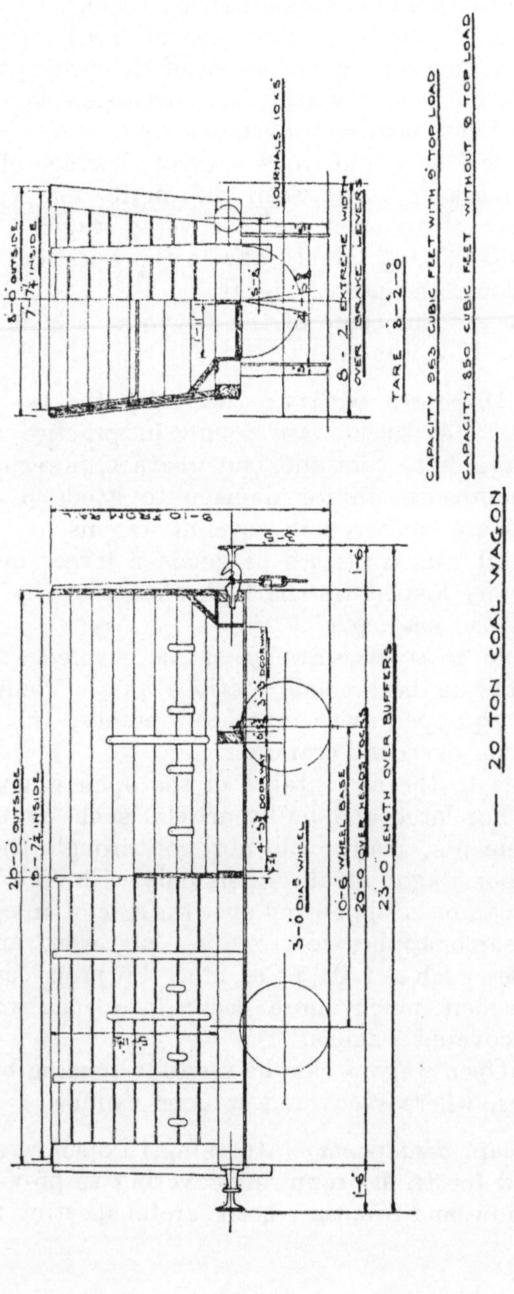
8-0 OUTSIDE
7-7¼ INSIDE
JOURNALS 10×5
8-2 EXTREME WIDTH
OVER BRAKE LEVERS
TARE 8-2-0
CAPACITY 963 CUBIC FEET WITH 9" TOP LOAD
CAPACITY 850 CUBIC FEET WITHOUT 9 TOP LOAD
20 TON COAL WAGON
20-0 OUTSIDE
19-7¼ INSIDE
3-0 DIA. WHEEL
10-6 WHEEL BASE
20-0 OVER HEADSTOCKS
23-0 LENGTH OVER BUFFERS
4-5½ DOORWAY
3-5 DOORWAY

FIG. 16.

purposes. The need for this was referred to when we dealt with the question of common user of wagons.

Having set out the dimensions of these various types, I would now mention two or three of the principal questions which will immediately arise for discussion as soon as the question of standardisation is taken up.

There will be found to be a great cleavage of opinion in the first instance as between the merits for general goods station user of an open and a covered wagon. The difference of wagon very largely affects the question of loading: it also affects the use of sheets.

Let me set out some of the advantages in favour of the covered or box wagon:—

1. Dispenses with the necessity for use of wagon sheets. As sheets are found in practice never quite impervious to rain and bad weather, fewer claims arise for compensation for damage to goods by wet when goods are conveyed in covered wagons.
2. Of mixed classes of goods a larger quantity can be safely loaded, as the higher sides of the box wagon assist the loading.

The one great *disadvantage* of the covered wagon is that in some of the best goods stations in the country, which are well equipped with overhead cranes, the covered in top prevents overhead craning.

Now as to the advantages of the open wagon:—

1. For large and bulky articles such as agricultural implements, many will not go through the doorway of a box wagon at all, others only with difficulty, whilst they can be easily swung over the side of an open wagon. The same applies to iron ore, pig iron, and lengthy articles, such as rails, poles, etc. Pit props can evidently be loaded much more easily into open wagons than into covered wagons.
2. Open wagons can be used for loading by overhead cranes, whereas covered wagons cannot.

The main *disadvantage* attaching to open wagons is that when used for traffic requiring covering to prevent damage by rail, snow, and fire, they need careful sheeting to keep out wet and fire which may result from a stray spark from an engine, and even the best of care does not prevent numerous claims arising from damage to goods in transit caused by wet. The perfect wagon cover which will always remain impervious to wet weather has not yet been discovered.

The pros and cons seem to be so balanced that the two types are bound to exist, but a general standard of each needs to be developed now that these individually owned railway wagons are used in common by all railway companies.

It is interesting to note that the railway companies of America have adopted the covered type of car for all their general goods station traffic : it is there called a " box-car," the other two principal types being the flat car, and the open or Gondola car ; but in that country an average load per wagon is from 25 to 30 tons. The growth of this average in recent years was dealt with in Chapter VI.

There has been much discussion as to the relative merits of 10 or 12 tons as the plated capacity of an ordinary open goods wagon, and as a result it is quite probable 12 tons will be the carrying capacity adopted. Let us consider. Many ordinary goods wagons are plated to carry 6, 7, or 8 tons to-day, and to fix 12 tons in place of these smaller figures seems to be a big step to take all at once towards a larger capacity wagon. Is it worth while incurring the extra cost of a 12 tons capacity wagon when there is some doubt as to whether as a 10-ton wagon it can ever or often be filled, the possible load often being only 3, 4, or 5 tons.

But the answer to this question must be found in the balancing of advantages of the larger wagon of a 12 ton capacity rather than 10 over against the extra cost involved, and the advantage of a still larger capacity wagon will in its turn depend on the frequency with which it could secure a load of 12 tons. Going back again to our illustrative mixed train (61 wagons), we see there were in that illustration two cases where the load exceeded 10 tons. Any station master or goods agent can tell how annoying it has been when he has had 11 or 12 tons of goods to forward in one consignment, he has found that two wagons must be used for the conveyance because the weight has been a fraction over the 10 ton capacity.

Two wagon loads out of 61 in a train perhaps does not seem to afford much justification for a 12-ton wagon, and we must examine the circumstances a little further. May not the fact of so few 12-ton loads be due partly to the very fact that wagons of this capacity were not available? Had they been, a very slight examination of the table will show that the 11 wagon loads of copper ore at the end of the list would have been comfortably conveyed in 9 wagons, and the same degree of saving could probably have been effected throughout the train.

Whether a 12-ton load can be secured for a wagon plated "to carry 12 tons" depends largely on the weight or specific gravity of the contents. Such a wagon may be loaded to its fullest capacity with hay and straw, or general goods, of not more than 4, 5, or 6 tons in weight, whilst if copper or iron ore or packed hams and bacon or potatoes are requiring conveyance the wagon will load fully up to its capacity.

Now as to the difference in construction which affects the original cost of the wagon. The factor of primary importance as affected by load in the running of a wagon is the safe and easy carriage of the load of the wagon on the axles or journals[1]: if a heavier load is to be carried, the journals must be stronger and of larger dimensions, and it will often be found that the only reason why 12 tons cannot be placed in a wagon is that it is only plated to carry 10: the journal has been the limiting factor. It may indeed be found that to adopt a standard 12-ton as against a 10-ton wagon for general merchandise, a stronger and larger journal (say 9 inches long by 5-inch diameter instead of 9 inches by 4 inches) and springs of greater bearing strength is all that is involved, and the cost of such additional or enlarged equipment would be small in percentage to the total cost of the wagon.

I am merely stating for students the considerations to which regard must be had before this question can be determined. An error may easily be made in an assumption that to increase the carrying capacity of a wagon from 10 to 12 tons would mean a *correspondingly* increased cost of construction and upkeep. It might mean this if the matter was

[1] The "journal" is that part of the axle which bears the load.

simply dependent on cubical capacity, but the fact that the rolling friction as affected by the weight borne upon the axles has to enter into the calculation makes the whole problem a much more intricate one.

A few of the principal points as affecting mineral wagons must now be referred to. Much discussion has taken place and much has been written upon the controversies involved in the following four questions :—

1. Is it practicable to adopt a general user wagon equally available for general goods and coal or ironstone ?

2. Ought mineral traffic to be conveyed in wagons privately owned by traders—the system largely in vogue to-day—or ought all the mineral wagons, as in the case of goods wagons, to belong to the railway companies ?

3. What is the best standard of equipment for discharge of coal traffic from the wagons—end doors, side doors, or bottom doors ?

4. What are the best weight standards of capacity for general adoption—10, 12, 15, 20, or 40 tons ?

Let us discuss the points involved in these questions one by one.

Is it practicable to adopt a general type of wagon available equally for general goods and coal or ironstone ?

Whilst to some extent it is the practice to-day to use railway companies' wagons which convey coal from the Midlands or from South Wales into London for goods going out from London, it has to be remembered that at present the bulk of the London coal is conveyed in privately owned wagons which are mostly returned empty to collieries : so that as a matter of fact coal wagons are very slightly made use of for other traffic than minerals.

Coal traffic is carried almost entirely in bulk in the wagons, and leaves much of its dust in the empty wagons, which is an argument often used against the after use of the wagons indiscriminately for goods, such as sacks of flour, bacon, fruit or vegetables ; but there are many classes for which they could be and are used, such as ores, roadstone, bricks, etc. During the war they were used generally for all classes of merchandise, but before being loaded with goods traffic they were well swept in order to prevent damage by coal dust, and it is the practice of some companies, in order to avoid empty haulage, to utilise their wagon stock indiscriminately for coal and goods traffic, due discretion being made as to the class of traffic loaded in the wagons after they have conveyed a load of coal.

Broadly speaking, the character of coal traffic is such as may call for the evolution of a special wagon : the loading of wagons at colliery screens, degree of curves and other factors affect the dimensions, whilst the facilities for the discharge of the contents (which are carried in bulk) must also have a large bearing on the construction of the wagon. The construction of a goods wagon is determined by quite other considerations.

As regards question 2, as to *whether private traders or the railway companies should own the stock of mineral wagons*, the question is too big to admit of anything like a full discussion in this chapter, and we can only point out the salient facts.

It is estimated that there are in the country about 1,400,000 railway wagons, of which about 650,000 belong to private owners, mostly coal or mineral wagons. Of the 650,000 privately owned wagons, 612,000 are under 12 tons capacity (Sir Eric Geddes in parliament July 7, 1919).

In the North Eastern Railway districts of Northumberland, Durham and Yorkshire, the coal traffic is carried in railway-owned wagons, and the company has been able to do more than any other to establish higher capacity wagons for this traffic. In 1922 the published figures of the North Eastern Railway showed a stock of 21,259 wagons of a 12 ton capacity out of a total stock of 123,823 wagons.

If a policy of increase in the capacity of mineral wagons is to be adopted in Great Britain, it would seem to be necessary that the wagons must be in the hands and ownership of the railways, so that the standards most suitable for use in conveyance on the railways may be devised and adhered to.

Any question of increased cost in construction or maintenance thrown upon present owners might be adjusted in the rates and charges on the traffic, though it is quite conceivable that the colliery owners may benefit by an enlarged wagon standard as much as the railway companies themselves. But in any event, as this controversy might be disposed of by an adjustment in charges on traffic, nothing ought to stand in the way of an improved standard of wagon which will so manifestly benefit and economise the working of traffic. The fact that the North Eastern Railway at present transports the whole of its Durham and Northumberland coal trade in railway-owned wagons is sufficient evidence that the problem of transfer of the wagon stock from private to railway ownership is a practicable one.

Wagon Doors and Methods of Discharge of Coal.—The method of discharge depends to a large extent on the destination of the traffic, and the facilities at and the construction of the wharves, depots, or receiving yards, and in case of export traffic upon the crane or tipping equipment at the port. At present some wagons have side doors, much like an ordinary goods wagon, some have end doors, some have bottom doors. With side-door wagons the coal is discharged much as with ordinary goods, and is usually stacked upon a cart or upon the ground in a goods or coal yard. In other cases, however, the coal requires to be discharged into cells or bins, where the wagon is taken on rails overhead, and the coal is tipped by gravity through a trap door in the bottom of the wagons. This description of bottom-door wagons is also necessary for shipping coal on the gravitation principle through spouts or shoots arranged on staging as in the staiths of many ports, especially in the North of England. This is the principle of shipment largely adopted on the Tyne, at Blyth, the Wear, and at Hartlepool. The wagon is brought vertically over the shoot, the doors are one by one opened out by the removal of a strong pin by "teemers," and the coal drops through the shoot (or spout) into the hold or bunker hatch of the vessel. The end-door wagon, on the other hand, is equally necessary for the method of shipment at many ports where the wagon and its contents are lifted bodily and swung by crane over the hold of the ship and then teemed through the wagon end which swings open and so forms a door. This method of end-door discharge is also adopted at Hull and on the south side of the Humber, where the wagon is elevated by hoist (hydraulic or electric), which, in combination with a shoot or spout, tips up the wagon in a semi-vertical position so as to discharge its contents through the end door, and so shoot them into the vessel's hold.

As many mineral wagons are required sometimes for one class of shipping and sometimes for another, a number have been constructed with both end and bottom doors, or end and side doors, or all three, so as to be available for use in whatever way required.

I have set out this brief outline of facts so that it may be realised that the particular type of wagon in this important matter of the description of door to be adopted cannot be determined without very careful consideration of the methods of discharging now in vogue and the particular appliances at each unloading point. The problem needs to be tackled in its entirety by the united intelligence of railway experts.

A summary of the present position of the capacities of railway-owned wagons is obtainable from the statistics in the railway companies' yearly reports, which show the proportion of wagons in four groups of capacity, viz.: (1) under 8 tons; (2) 8 tons up to 12; (3) 12 tons up to 20; (4) over 20 tons. These figures as regards thirteen of the largest companies which own more than seven-eighths of the railway wagons, are set out below, and it will be seen that the total number of wagons of capacity of more than 12 tons is 39,756, out of a total of 607,760, or 6½ per cent.:—

Year 1915.	Open Goods.	Covered Goods.	Mineral.	Total.
Under 8 tons	19,043	13,058	559	32,660
Over 8 and up to 12	334,547	65,984	134,813	535,344
Over 12 and up to 20 ..	2,982	776	34,524	38,282
Over 20 tons	140	159	1,175	1,474
Total	356,712	79,977	171,071	607,760

In this chapter on types of wagons something should be said in regard to "higher capacity" wagons. The innovation which the term suggests to some people savours of "Americanising our institutions," in the republic across the Atlantic so much has been done in the way of big wagon loads as in other big things. But we may leave America out of account for the time being and think only of our own requirements. In the 40,000 or so wagons which have been referred to as exceeding 12 tons in capacity the majority will consist of a 20-ton wagon, and that wagon has therefore fairly established its *raison d'être* as a useful British wagon under suitable circumstances.

By "high" capacity wagons in this chapter I mean therefore something of greater capacity still, and I shall refer simply to two types :—

(1) A 25-ton wagon for general goods traffic.
(2) A 40-ton wagon for coal.

High Capacity Covered (25 *Tons*) *Goods Wagon.*—Whilst this type of wagon may be useful for a backwards and forwards service between two large towns which have a constant exchange of general traffic, e.g. London and Bristol, London and Newcastle, gives a good tare ratio, it is too large for any general adoption other than as suggested. As has been already pointed out, this is the common type of wagon in use in America for all general goods, although the American unit is a still larger one, averaging about 42 tons capacity.

An illustration of an English wagon of this type is given on page 132 (Fig. 17). Its dimensions are as follows :—

Length over buffers	40 ft. 5 in.
Length over head-stocks..	37 ft.
Length of wheel-base	27 ft. (centre of bogie)
Length inside wagon	36 ft. 3 in.
Plated capacity of wagon	25 tons
Tare weight of wagon	15 tons
Dimensions of journals	9½ in. × 4¼ in.
Lubrication	Oil

Of these covered wagons for general goods it needs to be pointed out that the cubic capacity of the wagon will not usually admit of general goods being loaded up to anywhere near the plated capacity; for instance, a 12-ton covered wagon well filled with average consignments of mixed goods would probably not accommodate more than 5, 6, or 7 tons,

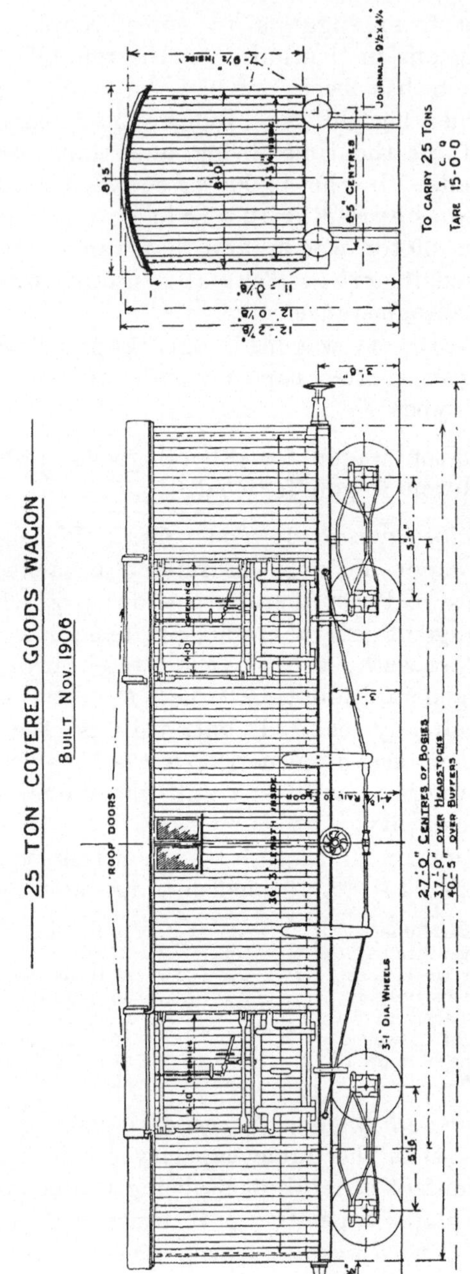

Fig. 17.—High Capacity Covered Goods Wagon: 25 Tons.

and its full capacity in weight would only be required for a cargo of specially heavy freight. Similarly, a well-loaded 25-ton wagon will rarely carry more than 10 or 12 tons.

Large Capacity (40 *Tons*) *Mineral Wagon.*—When a wagon is constructed to carry more than 20 or 25 tons, it is found necessary to place the wagon body on bogie trucks, and this immediately introduces complications in the relation between tare and contents weights, as the adoption of the "bogie" principle adds not a little to the weight of the wagon.

Hereunder are set out the dimensions of this wagon :—

Length over buffers	39 ft. 5 in.
Length over head-stocks..	36 ft. 7 in.
Length inside wagon	35 ft.
Plated capacity of wagon	40 tons
Tare weight of wagon	15 tons, 15 cwt.
Capacity (estimated)	1,800 cubic feet
Lubrication	Oil
Hand-screw brake.	

The sample wagon taken is that running on the North Eastern system in Northumberland.

In point of fact, it is only under exceptional circumstances that a wagon of this capacity can be employed, and we cannot advocate it as in any way a useful standard for adoption excepting under local conditions, where it can be introduced in a restricted area of working, as in the case of the large Northumberland collieries where it works to and fro as between colliery and shipping point for export coal. It is, however, a very good illustrative case to test the advantages that accrue when it can be adopted. It is worth while first to table the comparative weights and dimensions and earning capacity of three types of wagon, 10, 20, and 40 tons, and secondly to set out the advantages.

The following tables set out the gross weight and length of a train carrying 600 tons in the three different classes of wagon :—

	Gross Weight of Train.	Length of Train in Feet.
	Tons.	
In 60 10-ton wagons	975	1,170
In 30 20-ton wagons	810	690
In 15 40-ton wagons	780	591

These figures show that a much less heavy and costly engine could be used for the same load of traffic with higher capacity wagons, and much less siding room would be required for the standage or manipulation of the same quantity of traffic ; or, putting the matter in another way, the same engine and engine power cost could work a considerably heavier tonnage of traffic in the same gross weight of train. The following table will illustrate this in the case of an engine whose hauling capacity is taken at 1,000 tons in 10-ton wagons. If the wagons employed were 20-ton wagons, we may assume, owing to the more concentrated nature of the load, the engine capacity would be increased to at least 1,150 tons, and if 40-ton wagons were used to 1,225 tons, the resistance per ton diminishing with the concentration of load :—

Same Engine with Load in differing Wagons.	No. of Wagons on Train.	Actual Weight of Train.	Weight of Freight Carried.	Relative Earnings per Trip.	
				1s. per Ton.	7s. per Ton.
		Tons.	Tons.	£	£
1,000 tons in 10-ton wagons ..	62	1,000	620	31	217
1,150 tons in 20-ton wagons ..	42	1,134	840	42	294
1,225 tons in 40-ton wagons ..	24	1,248	960	48	336

I have specially mentioned, amongst the principal types of wagons, cattle wagons and timber wagons : these are a class of wagon which every railway company is bound to employ in considerable number, and I therefore give an illustration of a type wagon of each of these, Figs. 18 and 19. The timber wagon, generally known as a bolster wagon, is used for rough or "round" timber and lengthy traffic, the load being often carried over three, four, or five of these wagons when long tree-trunks or telegraph poles have to be dealt with. Of these bolster wagons there are two types, namely the "single" and "twin." The twin type is constituted by a fixed central swivel coupling attachment between two of a type (as shown in Fig. 19) similar to the single bolster wagons. The advantage of the "twin" over two "single" trucks is that they are closer coupled, thus

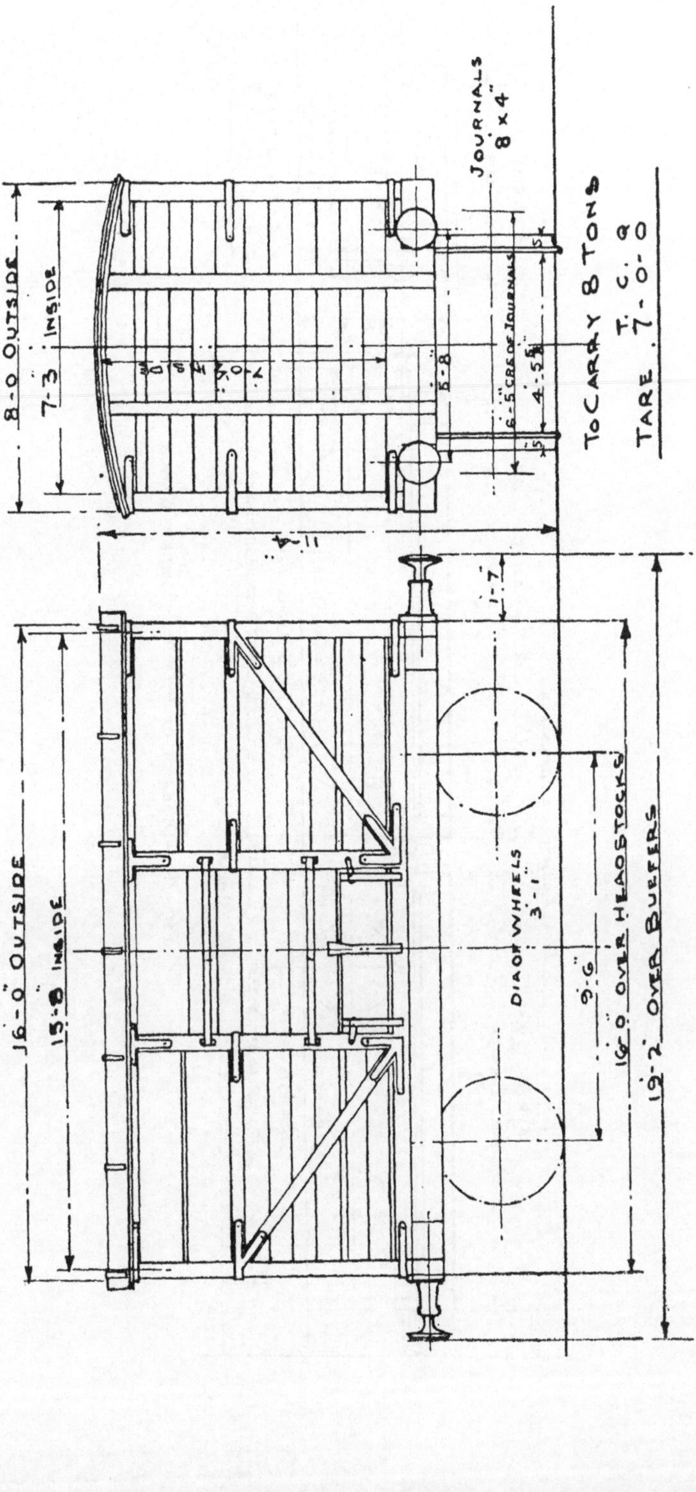

FIG. 18.—DIAGRAM OF CATTLE WAGON.

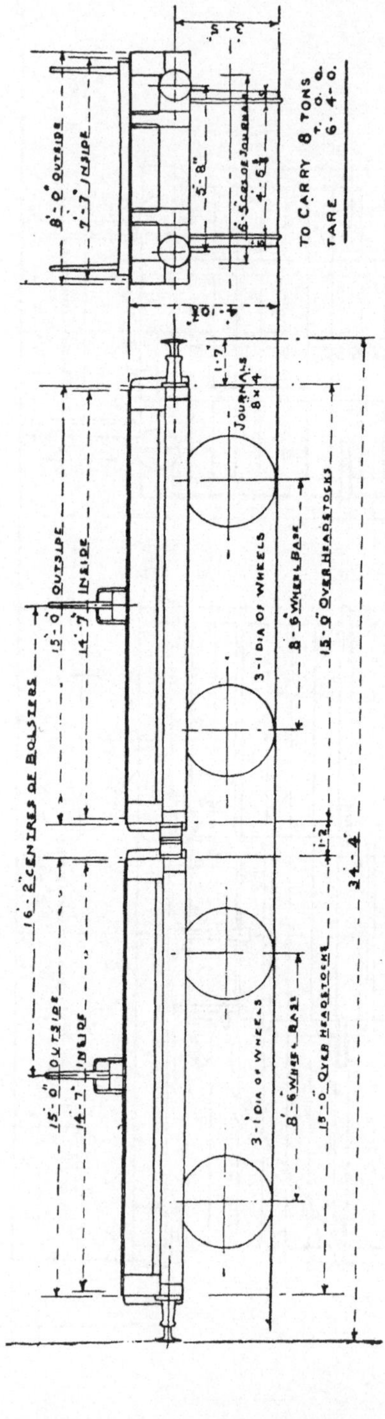

FIG. 19.—DIAGRAM OF "TWIN" TIMBER WAGON.

providing for less longitudinal movement in conveying a long article resting on the bolsters of the twin wagon. Some of the British railways have in recent years made considerable headway in the construction of timber stock, and have built high capacity bogie vehicles, as presenting a safer and more advantageous method in dealing with long and weighty traffic. These are generally 30-ton wagons, and can be used for such articles as long boilers as well as timber, long iron girders, etc. Experience has proved these to be most useful vehicles and much in demand.

We also enumerate some of the other classes of wagon which are of general use on the various railway systems, all of which will need to be considered in their turn when the general question of standardisation is seriously taken up for determination :—

Fish wagon (required to run on express or passenger train service).

Goods wagon, low-sided.

Road van, 10, 12 or 15 tons capacity.

Trolley wagons, 20, 30, or 40 tons capacity.

We conclude this chapter with a summary of the weight capacities of the principal wagons which have been dealt with, with the object of showing what is the percentage ratio of wagon tare to gross load :—

Description of Wagon.	Plated Capacity of Wagon.	Tare Weight.	Ratio of Tare to Gross Weight.
	Tons.	T. C. Q.	Per Cent.
Open goods wagon	12	6 9 0	34·1
Covered goods wagon ..	12	6 18 0	36·9
Covered goods wagon ..	25	15 0 0	37·5
10-ton mineral wagon ..	10	6 9 0	38·0
15-ton mineral wagon ..	15	7 11 0	33·5
20-ton mineral wagon ..	20	8 2 0	28·8
40-ton mineral wagon ..	40	15 5 0	28·3

In this table I have included a 15-ton mineral wagon for comparison purposes. It will be observed that there is a general tendeney to reduce tare ratio as the capacity of wagon increases.

It should be noted what an important part the wheel

journal and the lubrication plays in the capacity and satisfactory running of a wagon. A small dimension wagon with journals of less than 4 inches diameter should be prohibited from carrying more than 7 tons, whilst if larger journals are substituted, the wagon may be allowed to carry 10 tons when it can get such a load, and in the course of a year probably many such opportunities may occur. So with a high-sided open goods or a large covered wagon or any larger capacity wagon, it is important to have sufficiently large journals, or the load capacity, which might be 12 or more tons, will have to be kept down so as not to exceed 10.

The periodical complete overhaul which every wagon needs to undergo every two or three years at the hands of the builders will necessitate re-plating as to tare, and occasionally but rarely as to capacity : and the varying ages of wagons will account to some extent for the great diversity of plated tares upon wagons which appear to be of the same general standard. The other day the writer observed a train load of coal (42 wagons) all carried in 10-ton wagons of apparently the same standard, but their plated tare varied at every cwt. from 5–19–0 to 6–9–0.

The question of journals has been emphasised ; à propos of this question, that of the importance of lubrication must be referred to. Some years ago, with a view to ascertain the correct gradient on which wagons would run of their own momentum into sorting sidings, the writer and others undertook some experiments to examine the running capacities of a large number of different wagon types on a steep grade, some empty, some heavily laden. The principal result of this experiment was to convince those who witnessed it that lubrication is a matter of greater importance than any detail of wagon weight or construction, and is also the prime factor which determines the degree of gradient necessary. The superiority of oil over grease as a lubricant for easy running was abundantly justified.

The question of standardisation of wagons ought not to pass without some reference to brakes, for it is in regard to the brakes in use on goods wagons that there is perhaps more diversity of type than in any other direction. The handles sometimes point one way, sometimes the other ;

sometimes they are at the end of the wagons, sometimes at the side ; sometimes on both sides, more usually only on one ; they are of varied length and of differing shape. When it is remembered that during shunting operations on a down grade the prompt control of the wagon by its brakes on the part of the responsible shunter is as it were a " key " operation in expeditious yard working, the importance of having brakes of something like even or uniform type can be imagined.

The question of a uniform brake has, however, received no small attention at the hands of the experts and the Board of Trade authorities. In April 1906 a Departmental Committee was appointed to examine, and if found necessary to test, appliances designed to diminish danger to men employed in the railway service, and one of the first efforts of this committee was to find a uniform brake for goods wagons, and one which could be applied equally on either side of the wagon. As soon as expert consideration was given to the matter it was realised that a standard brake of this kind should be capable of being *released*, as well as applied, on either side of the wagon—which added enormously to the complexity of the problem. Much experimenting with all wagons at all likely to conform with what was required took place, and the committee made several reports as to how they were progressing. They ultimately recommended for adoption a certain set of rules, and the Board of Trade accepted the recommendation and gave public notice that they proposed to adopt the rules which were as follows :—

1. The levers to be " cross cornered," and so placed that each lever will be to the right of a man facing the wagon side.
2. The levers to be of light pattern.
3. The levers to be capable of being operated by one hand.
4. The levers to be " press down and lift up," and to be provided when in the " off " position with a stop.
5. The handles of the levers to be not less than 3 feet and not more than 3 feet 6 inches from the rail

level in the " off " position, and not less than 12 inches in the " on " position.

Exemption was provided for wagons of over 20 tons capacity and certain specially constructed vehicles.

Then an unexpected incident came in the way of the carrying out of this notice which was publicly issued by the Board of Trade. The Great Western Company opposed the proposals because they had themselves a brake in operation which did not conform to the new rules, but did carry out one of the main requirements, viz. that of being capable of application or of release on either side. The Great Western Railway's opposition of the Board of Trade proposals was heard before the Railway Commission, and that body gave a decision in favour of the railway company.

This was many years ago, but there the matter rests. It still awaits solution, and will doubtless be taken up amongst other questions of standardisation urgently requiring settlement in the interests of the railways.

We would venture to suggest that not only does the very great diversity of practice show a state of affairs hardly creditable to a country of such great resource as our own, in that it must mean a very great amount of waste time, as the variety of type alone creates difficulty for the working staff and makes against speed in movement; but more than this to those who are accustomed to the use of continuous brakes on goods trains our hand brakes in their multifarious patterns necessarily seem a little antiquated and out of date.

In America the whole of the goods cars operated on the railways of that country are fitted with continuous air brakes. Without attempting to balance the advantages and disadvantages of equipping with continuous brakes or of attempting any estimate of cost, it ought to be borne in mind that the great difference in the maximum speeds recognised on our railway systems as between goods and passenger trains turns more upon this question of an efficient brake than any other factor.

The question of speed, or rather slowness, of movement in the operation of freight traffic on British railways is having to get the consignment note filled up and signed, and he is supplied with a stock of blank documents for the purpose.

It should moreover be stated that as the sender is required to state (on the consignment note document) whether he himself or the consignee at the destination end is to pay the carriage charges, if he is paying in advance the carter or rulleyman is authorised to accept the money. Of course, in a great many cases it is impossible to do this when the goods are tendered to the carter, as the latter has no means of knowing what the carriage charges will be, and the cash side of the transaction has to be dealt with subsequently by the rulleyman or a collector appointed for the purpose. In the case of carriage charges being payable at the consignee's or receiving end, the general regulations of all companies are that the charges due are to be paid by the consignee before the goods are given up to receiver, unless the consignee has an authorised credit account with the railway company.

Having outlined the *modus operandi* in filling up a consignment note, it will be appropriate and convenient next to refer to and describe the meaning of the invoice, which is the official record of goods sent from one station to another. The word "invoice" is evidently closely related to the French word *envoyé,* i.e. sent with. The invoice is made out by the staff at the station from which the goods are despatched. When the goods have been placed into the wagon, the wagon number is inserted on the consignment note, and this document is taken from the point where the goods are loaded to the invoicing staff. Particulars showing the name of consignee and sender, with a description of the goods, the weight and wagon number are copied from the consignment note on to an invoice form, the chargeable rate at which the goods are to be conveyed is inserted and the charges to which the company is entitled for services rendered is entered in either the "paid" or "to pay" column of the invoice; in the "paid" column when the sender pays the charges, and the "to pay" column when they are to be collected on delivery of the goods to the consignee. The invoice should either be sent along with the goods to the receiving station bulk, ironstone, etc., charged at very low rates per ton per mile ; whilst Class 5 embraces the more valuable goods which will bear higher rates, such as seal-skins, etc., other descriptions of goods falling between these two extremes. These rates, which are all tabled in parallel columns in the rate-books, are known as the "class rates" ; but the great fact behind the rates system in Great Britain is that all the more important traffic which passes by rail is not conveyed at those class rates at all, but at a special or "exceptional rate" specifically arranged by the goods manager for the traffic in question. Whenever traffic passes in any quantity, the sender applies to the railway company for an exceptional rate, and usually gets one quoted, and it is the recording of these exceptional rates, along with the class or ordinary rates, that constitutes the principal complication of our rate-book system. The exceptional rates seem to have become the rule in our British rates system.

The rates for the heavy traffics under A, B, and C (classes A and B are sometimes spoken of as "mineral class") are quoted by the railway company as "station to station" (S. to S.), which signifies that the trader must bring his own goods to the station at the forwarding end and take delivery at the receiving station, so doing his own cartage. A minimum weight per consignment is attached to these classes, in the case of A and B 4-ton lots, and C 2-ton lots, and where this is not maintained higher charges are made. On the other hand, the other five classes—1, 2, 3, 4, and 5—include traffic for which the railway companies are prepared to perform the service of cartage to and from the stations at each end in those places where they have cartage teams of their own, and for all such traffic the rates are noted and quoted accordingly under the abbreviated description "C and D" (that is to say "collected and delivered").

There is one other important condition which is attached to practically all rates, under the letters C.R or O.R.—"company's risk" or "owner's risk" alternatively. There are certain articles and commodities, such for instance as those that are of an explosive or dangerous or of a very easily damageable nature, which the railway companies will only carry at the owner's risk ; whilst on the other hand it is the general practice to have two rates for many commodities, the normal rate carrying with it the normal risk which attaches to the carrier, that is the normal rate is a C.R. rate ; but a second and lower rate is allowed by the company and stands on their books as an O.R. rate, and is applied when the sender or owner of the goods signs a risk note to the effect that he will himself bear the cost of any loss, damage, or depreciation arising to his goods in connection with their journey or conveyance : wilful negligence on the part of the agents of the company is generally excepted from this condition of owner's risk.

3. To see that "Inward" Goods are Properly Delivered to the Consignee or Receiver. This is a comparatively simple matter, and has already been shortly described. When the goods have arrived at their station of destination, as they are unloaded they again need to be carefully checked to see (1) that they are intact and in good condition, and (2) that they agree with the particulars recorded on the invoice ; they are then sorted out on to the rulley destined for the various districts of the town at which they have arrived. As each rulley load of goods is made up, a sheet is made out on which is listed the goods on the rulley with the names of the consignees and the address of the premises at which they are to be delivered, and particulars of any charges to be collected. This document has already been referred to as the "Delivery Sheet," and contains a column headed "Signature of Consignee" ; and as each parcel of goods is handed over to its due consignee, a signature of the latter or his agent is taken with a declaration that the goods are received in good and satisfactory condition, or otherwise. If anything is wrong or unsatisfactory in the condition of the goods, the recipient will make a remark accordingly on the delivery sheet document and add his initials.

As has already been pointed out, the company's agent who delivers the goods—the carman or rulleyman—is expected to collect any charges due on the carriage of the consignment before he parts with the goods, except in cases where a credit account has been granted by the railway company.

At small stations where the company have no rulleyman or carting agent to deliver the goods, the regular practice is to advise the consignee by postcard immediately on the arrival of the goods and request him to fetch the goods from the station within a definite and specified period.

4. To see that Goods Despatched by Rail are put on Truck in as Economical Manner as Possible, and that they are so Loaded as to Secure Expeditious Conveyance.

In the complex but interesting duties and responsibilities attaching to the staff of a goods station there are, although there is a general gradation of work and overlapping of services, certain broad lines of demarcation on organisation which it is essential to observe. We have already referred to certain of these, as for instance the distinction between C. & D. and S. to S. traffic, and the distinction between operating and commercial responsibilities, but we must refer to these in further detail.

The distinction between C. & D. and S. to S. traffic is a fundamental distinction affecting the handling of the traffic throughout. At most town stations the railway company maintains a staff of horses and carts, often spoken of as "teams," and where the railway company has such an agency or service they undertake the collecting of goods from the traders' premises to the station, and the corresponding delivery at the destination end of the journey. But the heavy classes of goods do not come under this provision, and any commodities in respect of which only the S. to S. rates are quoted (it includes all such goods as coal, coke, lime, timber, salt, sand, and very often flour and grain) are loaded by the sender's agents in the sidings in the goods yard as distinguished from the actual station building—not uncommonly but very inappropriately called a goods "warehouse." There is not the same need for covered accommodation for this heavy class of traffic as in the case of the more general consignments.

Another important line of demarcation deeply affecting organisation in the service of transportation of goods is that in respect of the terminal and conveyance portion of the journey. The goods station stands on the frontier between the one service and the other. The business of railway transport is to move goods from sending to receiving point ; the actual conveyance by railway train from one station to another is what is technically known as the "conveyance" service. It commences when the goods have been placed in the wagon and are ready for despatch, and is brought to completion when the goods are taken out of the wagon at the destination end. As regards accommodation, the rolling stock (i.e. the locomotive power and the wagon) and the permanent way are covered in the term "conveyance"; the station itself and practically all its appurtenances and facilities are regarded as "*terminal*" facilities and accommodation; and all the services, carting, invoicing, loading, etc., incidental to the station work are terminal services (see diagram, page 160).

In the development of our large towns which involve such a large aggregation of goods day by day for despatch by rail, the question of terminal facilities and the best and most efficient method of handling goods at the terminals becomes a very important and, indeed, a highly technical one. This particular work of handling goods in a goods station divides itself between the moving of goods from point to point in the station itself and the actual placing or packing of them in the trucks in which they are to be conveyed. Both of these operations require experience and lend themselves to mechanical or technical treatment. They are treated departmentally in different manner by different railway companies.

We must now explain what is meant by the distinction, several times spoken of, between the operating and commercial functions on a railway company's system. The railway manager in his dealing with the transportation of goods has to see that adequate arrangements are made for the conveyance of his client's—the trader's goods. They must be both efficient from the point of view of giving the trader a good service ; they must be economical from the company's point of view.

In selling transportation to his customers or clients, i.e. the traders, the goods agent is standing between the technical operation of freight conveyance and the commercial function; when the goods come into the possession of the company and the agent devotes his attention to loading and despatch of the goods he is entering upon the business of technical transportation, and exercising an operating function. The distinction between operating and commercial is a difference of function which underlies the organisation of a railway company in its departments. It is more rigidly observed in America than it is here in England; but, broadly speaking, the general superintendent and his district assistants have charge of the functions of operating, whilst the commercial service comes under the goods manager and the various goods agents.

Another important line of demarcation exists between the clerical staff and goods shed staff—between clerks and porterage staff; but careful analysis will show that this is very much the same distinction as between commercial and operating, or rather it is the application of the principle which we have been speaking about in the abstract and with reference to the functions of the agent, to the human or staff arrangements at the station.

It is time now that we dealt with the specific operation of loading at the goods stations which from the operating point of view is its main, or at any rate most important, function. The whole of the arrangements of a goods station are as we analyse them carefully practically subservient to the one function of securing that goods brought to the station for conveyance by rail may be so loaded as to secure the most efficient and economical conveyance, and the general design of every station should be directed to this end. We have seen in previous chapters how important is the question of the train load and efficient loading in its bearing on economical railway operating, and we must now examine in detail the internal organisation of a goods station so that we may see how its general design tends to provide satisfactory loading facilities, and what a large scope is provided for the loader and his colleagues to contribute by securing good wagon loads to a great and continuous improvement in train working.

We have emphasised the functions of the loader at a

goods station. He is really a differentiated porter, or he may be better described as a skilled man who has gained skill from his experience and has been evolved in the course of time from the porter's grade.

Let us now describe the various grades in the personnel of the goods station staff. They are: (1) the foreman; (2) the checker; (3) the loader; (4) the goods porter or barrowman.

Briefly and succinctly the operation which is carried out at a goods station is as follows:—

> When the goods are received they are passed over the "scale" or weighing machine under the eye of a receiving agent, who may be a foreman, scalesman, or checker, and after being weighed they are taken under his orders, by hand-barrow by a porter, or by electric or mechanically driven truck, to the particular wagon in which the goods are to be loaded; or if the wagon is not in readiness for the goods, they are left at the appointed berth or stage point to await loading.

Usually a wagon is in readiness for the goods, and at the wagon side, or within the wagon, the porter hands over the goods to the loader, who stows the goods in the wagon in such a way as will secure safe transit and at the same time will give as big tonnage in each wagon as possible, the checker checking the goods into the wagon with the consignment note.

The loader by long practice becomes expert in his profession, and when the great variety of goods which may be destined for one destination is taken into consideration—a consignment of bacon, a perambulator, wire coils, paper, horseshoes, a piano and other furniture, for instance—the reader may picture how skill and experience come in to so pack the goods that injury by chafing or jolting during shunting and train running shall be avoided: an efficient loader may easily get half as big a load again as an unskilled man, apart from any question of loss by damage and breakage that ensues from inefficient or careless loading. (See "Loaders and Loading," Chapter VII.)

The actual organisation of any goods station is of necessity dependent in considerable measure upon the general lay-out of the station, and goods stations have lately been considerably modified by the adoption and installation of power cranes (electric or hydraulic) and other appliances for giving mechanical assistance in the movement of goods or wagons. But we will now take one of the simplest typical stations and explain the general working.

Within the goods station or shed (see diagram, Fig. 20) are three divisions of floor area: (1) the loading bench or platforms which is about 4 feet above the roadway level; (2) the roadway itself for approach or access by carts and rullies bringing traffic for despatch; and (3) the railway access between the parallel benches of the station on which the wagons enter and leave the shed. This will be seen by reference to the diagram.

Assume that at a London station the goods are for Manchester. The receiver will direct the porter to the "Manchester" berth or to berth No. 27. It is now being very generally found a convenient plan to number the loading berths consecutively, a number representing a particular destination—thus Manchester will be known as 27, Leicester 26, and so on. In a large station where there may be perhaps a hundred destinations, the consecutive number system provides its own key for the porter to discover his required berth, whereas the name Manchester or Leicester might require some hunting up in the case of a substitute or new hand.

We must now say a word or two about the checking process which furnishes the checker with the name by which his grade is known. When the goods arrive at the station, whether they come by the railway company's teams or by a private carter, they are, as already explained, accompanied by a consignment note which is the sender's declaration as to the nature of the goods he is despatching. The business of the checker is to see in the first instance that the goods correspond with the declaration on the consignment note, that the number of the packages coincide, and that the weight is properly stated. He must also carefully inspect the goods to see that they are in good condition, and well packed. If they are received in a damaged condition, he reports the

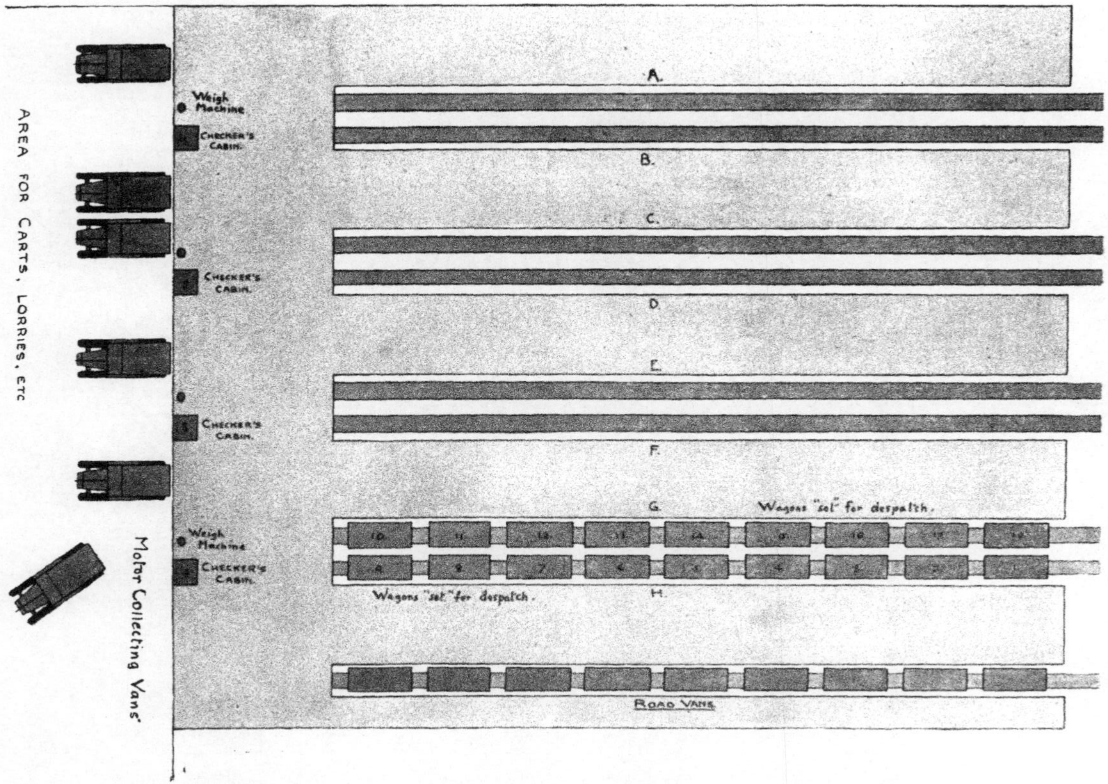

Fig. 20.—Diagram Showing Arrangement of Loading Benches and Wagons "Set" for Loading at a Goods Station.

matter to his foreman or to the office staff. Similar action must be taken if the goods are badly packed. If the sender insists on sending goods which appear to the company's agent to be likely to come to grief in transit owing to insecure packing, the checker will immediately bring the matter under the notice of his superior, who may refuse to allow the goods to travel.

To the loader's duties we have already referred in describing the process of loading; how complex this process is, and what a variety of methods and operations are involved we have seen in the chapter on "Loaders and Loading," and here a very short reference to the loader himself will be all that is necessary. The loader loads and the porter does the barrowing. The distinction is a very definite one. The loader, in a well organised station, has charge of a specific wagon or a number of wagons, and is responsible for receiving the goods from the barrowman, placing them in their right position in the wagon, and so packing them or stowing them that good loading is secured. When a wagon is completed with a full load he should be prepared to give a certificate that the wagon is properly loaded and will travel securely. A common practice is to require the loader to make out on a slip of paper a list of the goods loaded in his wagon, so that these particulars may be sent to the invoice clerk who has to insert the wagon number on the invoice. At well arranged stations the loader is required to make out a list of the goods in the wagon *with the weight of each package*, and a total giving the aggregate weight of the contents of the wagon.

As to the porters or barrowmen: their duty and service consists in moving the goods intended for conveyance from point to point in the goods shed as required; they constitute the rank and file in the goods station, and it is usually from their ranks that the loader and checker is appointed, and often the checker succeeds to the position of sub-foreman or foreman as any vacancy in the ranks of the latter grade occurs. The staff is usually divided into gangs under the leadership of a checker—a checker, three, four, or five porters, and a loader working as one gang.

The checker, loader, and porter are controlled by a foreman, who under the direction of the agent really is looked upon as being responsible for the smooth and efficient working of the goods shed. Where the shed staff is under the supervision of the general superintendent, the foreman comes under the direction of the yard-master.

There are other grades besides those named above employed in the working of a goods station, but the above-named represent the standard organisation. Modification and differentiation take place in accordance with local conditions or the size and volume of traffic dealt with. Where for instance hydraulic power and capstan working are in vogue there will be capstanmen ; at some stations the checker employs an assistant who is in charge of the weighing machine and known as a scalesman ; not uncommonly at the larger stations a "caller-off" is employed to call off the goods as the checker checks them over ; and "rulley checker" is a term used at some stations for the man who is employed to check goods as they are loaded on to a rulley for delivery.

I have referred to inwards and outwards traffic as being a main line of demarcation in goods station working ; so much is this so that at some places the inwards traffic is dealt with at one section of the station and the outwards at another, there being to all intents and purposes two stations almost independent of one another. (For instance the Midland Railway Station for despatch or forwarding of traffic from London is Somerstown, the station for inwards or received traffic is St. Pancras—separate stations, though practically adjoining.)

More commonly, however, the same station is used for both forwarded and received traffic, and in such cases the method will be for the station to be employed with received or inwards traffic in the morning from quite early on according to circumstances until nearly mid-day, the afternoon and evening generally being employed with forwarded or outgoing traffic. The exigencies of commerce are such that this arrangement is capable in most cases of convenient application. The two or three hours in the middle of the day between the arrival of the morning traffic and the despatch of the afternoon traffic by rail are utilised for cleaning up the station benches and "setting" the station lines and wagons for the afternoon's despatch work. This setting of the wagons is a matter of no small importance, and has to be arranged with the yard-master or the authority who has control of the wagon working in the district.

Continuous experience enables the foreman in charge to determine with a large amount of accuracy the various towns or destinations which are justified by traffic considerations in having wagons allocated, and where there is a large traffic the number of wagons for each place; and there will always at the beginning of the despatching period of the day be wagons "set" for a number of tranship points, as well as for specific destination stations.

Something must be said as to the general design of a goods station from the point of view of cranes or other labour-saving appliances. Many old-fashioned goods stations have a number of fixed cranes on the platforms erected on the principle that plenty of crane accommodation readily at hand is bound to be an advantage. As a matter of fact such fixed cranes on the platforms generally stand right in the fairway or gangway which should be kept clear for the barrowmen to pass up and down with their loads. The writer noticed on a visit to America how practically all the American goods stations exhibit an entire absence of cranes on the platforms, which in most cases at the period of goods despatch are alive—looking often as busy as a disturbed ant-hill—with the passage backwards and forwards of porters with their barrows and barrow loads.

The cranes should be so devised as to enable them to be used for lifting the goods from the lorries to the warehouse stage or direct to the wagon, and vice versa, in order to save duplication of handling. Heavy goods requiring crane accommodation should be dealt with in the yard rather than in the goods station building.

But the advent of overhead electric crane accommodation is destined to revolutionise goods station working at our large stations. With an installation of overhead travelling cranes running the whole length of the station with a transverse jib, a maximum of lifting and moving power can be provided without in any way encroaching upon the platform or bench accommodation. This is the system which has been installed at Oldham Road Station on the L. & N.W. system at Manchester, where the station consists of eight parallel bays or benches, over each one of which runs from end to end of the station a travelling crane with a transverse jib, so that it can be brought into action at any point along the line of rails, and can be used to lift goods laterally from cart to bench and bench to truck, or vice versa, the two motions—transverse and longitudinal—being made when necessary concurrently.

It must not be thought that the provision of such up-to-date electric power appliances is likely to do away with the barrowing or portering on the benches. There is a continuous succession of operations in the way of movement which require bench trucks or barrows. But in a goods station which has sufficient space for it a vast improvement can be effected by the application of electric or other power to the barrows or "truckers"—as they are called at Oldham Road Station, where they are employed with great effect.

Such a station, equipped with overhead cranes, and with a liberal supply of electric truckers at work on the benches, presents at a busy period of the day a most animated appearance. The human unit at work is an impressionable agency easily affected by environment, and there is good authority for the statement that in a well equipped station where inanimate machinery is constantly moving at a rapid pace it has (unconsciously to those affected) a quite considerable influence in quickening the speed of movement of every person working in the station. The life and movement of the whole place is quickened.

The work of a railway system has by some authorities been divided between that of movement when goods are in course of conveyance, and the fixed and stationary work at the terminal stations; in other words, it has been described as dynamic and static—these terms referring generally speaking to what is known in railway parlance as conveyance and terminal service respectively. But in transport everything is moving, and the more we look into the work of a goods station the more we shall see it is full of life and movement. The movement within a goods station may show less speed than that of conveyance on the railway, and the distance within the station is more circumscribed; but in a large modern goods station there is almost endless opportunity for speeding up, either by new and improved appliances, or by a more vigorous application of human energy in dealing with the work entailed. At a goods station, as with conveyance arrangements, there should be constant movement : goods should not accumulate. A goods station is not a "warehouse," though it sometimes is erroneously given that name. It is in reality a transit shed or building where goods are brought in to be immediately sent forward by rail, or the converse when goods are received by rail and sent on to consignee as quickly as possible.

The railway station is nevertheless the terminal of the consignment's journey by rail : and in view of the importance of understanding what is the exact relation of terminal to conveyance, we may make use of the diagram on the following page (Fig. 21).

Let us assume a consignment of goods passing from "A" to "B." It will be brought to the station either by the sender's or by the company's carting agent. From a theoretical point, in the interior of the station "conveyance" proper begins—in practice this is when the consignment is loaded on to the wagon and this is ready to be hauled away—and the vertical lines at each end "A" and "B" may be said to mark the frontier between terminal and conveyance in respect of which the railway company is entitled to make separate charges.

The efficiency of the organisation in a goods station depends mainly upon the personnel, and where there are so many and such diverse functions, it is of the utmost importance that every man should have his own proper work clearly defined. Whilst normally a porter will be barrowing, and a loader will be loading, there will be times (holidays, sickness, or emergency working) when the loader may have the opportunity and be expected to do higher grade work. But co-operation between all members of the staff in a goods station with a mutual feeling of goodwill and a desire to make the work of the station as a whole a credit to all concerned and a really efficient piece of machinery in the service of the commonwealth, is the greatest asset that any station can possess, and the surest

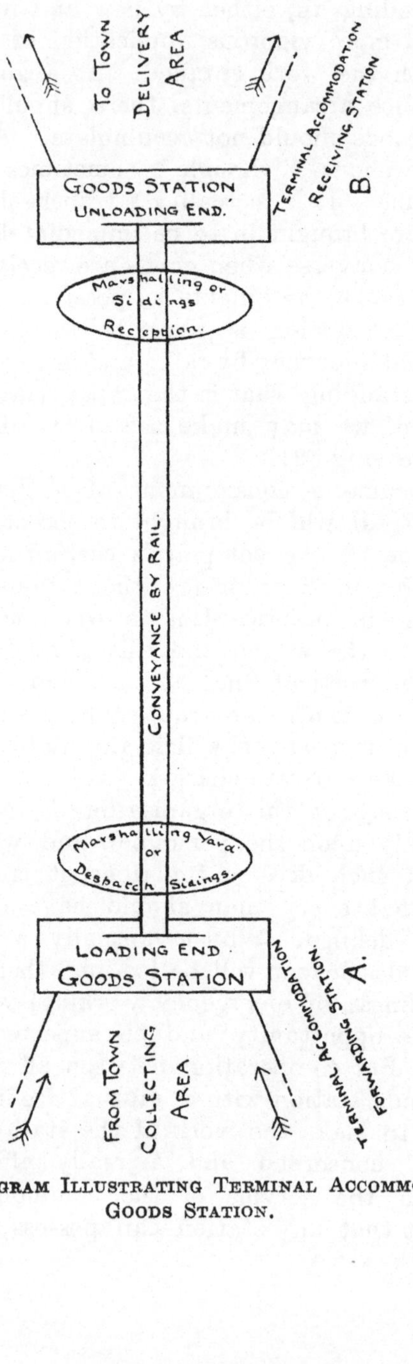

Fig. 21.—Diagram Illustrating Terminal Accommodation at Goods Station.

guarantee of satisfactory results. This has been already insisted on.

I have so far said little or nothing of the foreman who may be employed at the station. The goods station as a whole, along with the sidings in the station yard, will all come under the supervision of a yard-master, inspector, or chief foreman, who will require as his next lieutenants one or two foremen for the special supervision of the station working. There will probably be one foreman for the "forwarded" or down side or section of the station, and one for the "received" or up side; there may have to be three foremen for three eight-hour shifts if the station is continuously open. The foreman on duty will act as a go-between or nexus between the general supervision of the yard-master, inspector, or chief foreman, and the checkers amongst whom the actual executive work of the station is divided; but the arrangement of foremen's duties will necessarily depend upon the local environment and physical conditions.

It may be taken as a general rule that the more efficiently the checkers, loaders, and the rank and file carry out individually their several executive functions, the less need there will be for the foreman's intervention in the daily carrying on of the functions that the goods station is designed to give effect to.

Statistics.—Before concluding this chapter on the goods station some reference ought to be made to the statistics used to enable the agent to see whether the work at his station is being economically carried on. The agent will require to see daily statistics showing—

> The amount of tonnage and number of wagons forwarded.
>
> The amount of tonnage and number of wagons received.
>
> Number and cost of staff employed.

From these he will get a measure of the cost per ton in dealing with the traffic, also the average load per wagon, a most important unit which has been fully dealt with in the chapter (VI) on wagon loads. He will also require to have placed before him daily information showing the weight and cost of cartage (collection and delivery services), quantity of traffic left over at close of work on the previous day, times of arrival and departure of trains, and, although mentioned lastly, by no means the least important unit, the man-hours per ton and cost incurred in dealing with the goods by those grades of employees designated as "handling staff."

The wages cost of handling traffic is obtained by dividing the total amount of wages paid to the handling staff at the station by the total tonnage of traffic handled. Whilst this figure shows the *wages cost* per ton, it does not necessarily show the increased efficiency of the human units employed in output (or tons handled) per man, and for this purpose the actual tons dealt with must be divided by the number of men employed or by the number of "man hours" occupied upon the work. Any change in the rate of wages will obscure the result in reduced cost per ton brought about by increased energy or industry on the part of the workers, in comparison between one period with another. As regards comparison between one station and another, this source of obscuration does not apply, and comparisons of cost per ton of goods in different parts of the country or at stations where varying methods of dealing with traffic apply may often prove instructive, and suggestive of ways of improvement at the stations which show less economical results.

CHAPTER XI

TRANSHIPPING

It is only within recent years that the importance of an efficient and well-designed system of transhipping has been fully recognised by the British railway companies. The larger the railway system the greater is the need and the greater the scope for economy. Upon every system there are large towns between which good wagon loads can be secured without difficulty, as e.g. Manchester and Leeds, Derby and Bristol, London and Newcastle. But when one of the termini between which a small consignment has to be sent is a country village or a comparatively small town, and there is no regular stream of traffic, the obtaining of a good load under ordinary circumstances is a difficulty.

It is a difficulty which, though it cannot be altogether removed, may, by a proper system of transhipping, be very largely minimised.

In no country in the world probably is the trader more impatient or urgent in his demands to get his goods through to their journey's end quickly than in Great Britain, and an old rule or practice exists that where a minimum of a ton can be loaded in a wagon to one destination, a wagon may be sent through to destination. This internal arrangement between railway companies ought now to be re-considered; the minimum quantity is too low—one ton of freight in a wagon the tare of which is 5, 6, or 7 tons! By a regularised system of transhipping the consignment can now be ensured a through journey without delay. If 20 cwt. of goods is going through from London to Skipton (Midland Railway) in Yorkshire, and instead of going in a separate wagon through to Skipton it be combined with four or five other consignment loads of similar weight also going beyond or as far as Leeds "for transhipment at Leeds," it is probable that at Leeds it will fall into line with other consignments from other places—Nottingham, York, Chesterfield, also destined for Skipton, with the result that instead of five or six wagons with very light loads from London to Leeds and beyond, one well-loaded wagon will suffice, and from Leeds forward to Skipton also a well-loaded wagon is secured as against two or three or more lightly loaded wagons.

But the forwarding trader does not readily give up the *apparent* advantage of having his light load sent in a through wagon. Unfortunately, under our absurdly exaggerated competitive system, the rule of a through wagon for one ton minimum load, which was adopted as an internal railway regulation, was used as a canvassing weapon to secure traffic by a specific route, and came to be regarded by a trader almost as a matter of right. Under the *régime* of competitive canvassing it was a great temptation to a canvasser to be able to promise a forwarding trader that if he would make up a load of 20 cwt. to any specific point he should have a wagon reserved all to himself and for his own traffic, and the wagon should be sent through without any transfer of the goods at junction stations. The practice clearly needs reconsideration.

The complexity—as well as the way towards simplification—of this problem of transhipping will be most readily seen and appreciated by diagrammatic treatment (Fig. 22).

Let L (say Leeds or London) represent an important forwarding station at the south terminal of the railway system shown on the diagram ; amongst many other stations it has traffic in small consignments daily, not only to the towns A, B, and C, which are probably important receiving centres as well as junctions, but also for D, D1, D2, D3, D4, E, E1, E2, E3, F, G, H, I, J, and S, S1, S2 and S3 ; O and P, M and N on the diagram are also forwarding towns of some traffic importance, and they have consignments continually for the same destinations. They may or may not be on the same system of railway as L.

At A the three streams of traffic begin to converge from L, from M, and from N, as well as from O and P. There are also some diverging points—to O, to P, to E, and to the subsidiary stations beyond E. Similarly at B there are branch lines to S and F, and to T and E. Traffic to and from these stations on the branch lines leaves or comes into the main stream of traffic at B.

Now, it has been found by experience that A, B, and C are the points to which the natural concentration of traffic is such that there is a sufficient volume to enable

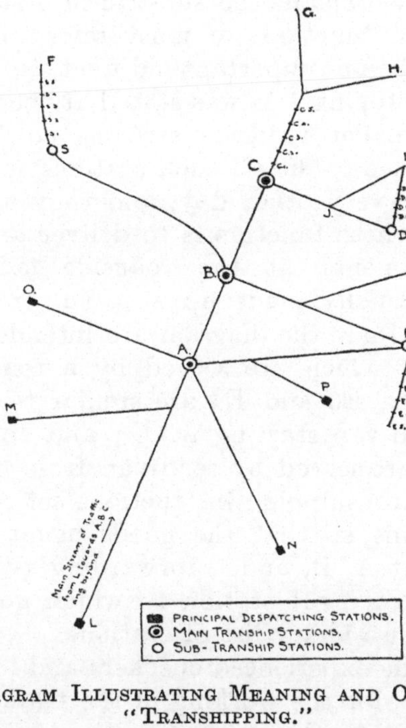

FIG. 22.—DIAGRAM ILLUSTRATING MEANING AND ORGANIZATION OF "TRANSHIPPING."

a sorting out of consignments to be so arranged as to provide good loads of traffic for wagons for various destinations, such as O, P, E (from A), S, T, F, K, E (from B), and D, G, H, I (from C). Instructions are therefore given to L, to M, and to N that all traffic in small consignments—less than 1 ton or 2 tons, or whatever weight may be decided upon—is to be loaded to the junction station A, B, or C, as the case may require for transhipment to destination. A, B, and C are termed "Main Tranship Stations."

In this way the whole of a railway system is mapped out under appropriate transhipping stations, and each railway system in the country having devised and catalogued its stations under various sections each with its main tranship stations (and a certain number of sub-tranship stations—see next paragraph) transmits its instructions to each of the other forwarding railway companies so that the whole country is co-ordinated for transhipping purposes.

We must now explain the sub-tranship stations, and to understand their function we must refer to the road-van system, which is an important adjunct to any complete system of transhipping. It was stated at the outset that for many of the smaller roadside stations *good* wagon loads cannot be obtained ; but all such stations must have their service daily or every other day, and they are best served by a road-van whose function is to deliver and pick up the smaller consignments at the roadside stations. These road-vans are usually made up at a sub-tranship station. D1, D2, D3, and D4 in the diagram are intended to represent roadside stations which are served by a road-van starting from D ; E1, E2, E3 and E4 are similar roadside stations served by a road-van starting at E ; and similarly S1, S2, S3, S4, and S5 are served by road-van from S.

The general transhipping instructions set out in detail all these explanations, so that the goods agent or chief foreman in charge at A, B, and C forwarding tranship stations knows precisely each sub-station to which goods should be loaded and the subsidiary list of stations.

In practice the experienced checkers and loaders who are daily responsible for the working of the traffic get to know without reference to the printed instructions exactly how each consignment should be loaded and worked, but the printed instructions are always kept at hand for the enlightenment of new members of the staff, or for guidance in the case of consignments for unaccustomed destinations, and the instructions are usually accompanied by explanatory maps.

If we may summarise these instructions, keeping in mind the opportunity which the individual loader at a station has before him in the arrangement of his wagon loads, he is presented with the following alternatives : (1) to load 2 tons through to destination in one wagon ; (2) to load 2 tons or more in one wagon to a sub-tranship station for stations within the zone or area of the particular sub-tranship station ; (3) to load to a main tranship station 2 tons or more of goods for stations served by such main tranship station ; (4) if none of the above alternatives can be adopted owing to the consignments not aggregating the necessary weight of 2 tons, load up the consignment in the road-van which passes the originating station and is bound for the nearest transhipping station in the hope and expectation that at such transhipping station other consignments will accumulate so as to render it possible to obtain a good wagon load out of the accumulated consignments.

Now let us consider how, in practice, the instructions are worked which enable a loader, say at Hertford, to select the proper wagon into which to load 15 cwt. of goods for Appleby (Westmorland).

The goods agent at Hertford, not having as much as 2 tons to forward to Appleby and so load in a through truck and ticket the wagon to destination, must refer to the *Tranship Instruction Book* for traffic to the North Eastern system. He will find there that Darlington is the main tranship station for Appleby, and if he can load 2 tons or more of mixed traffic to Darlington, he will make up a wagon of tranships and label the wagon to Darlington, for the Central District of the N.E.R., for which Darlington is a tranship station. If, however, he has not 2 tons for Darlington tranship station, he may make up a wagon of 2 tons of traffic to any stations on the North Eastern Railway and label the wagon to York. If this alternative fails owing to the agent at Hertford not having in the aggregate as much as 2 tons to the North Eastern District, he would then send to the most advantageous tranship station on his own system under local (Great Northern) instructions.

Each railway company now has its own scheme and instructions in regard to transhipping traffic, and every company sending traffic to another railway system recognises by mutual arrangement the tranship instructions of the railway company at the receiving end.

It will easily be recognised, in view of these somewhat complex instructions and the careful training that the station staff must have in regard to correct loading and routing of goods, that when wagons are loaded at a private trader's siding, some difficulty may occur.

It may seem on first thoughts that it is only necessary to train up the trader's loading agent by a special education to an understanding of all the regulations of the railway company in the matter of loading, or perhaps the railway company may lend a loader or checker for the purpose of directing the despatch in proper wagons. But these first thoughts clearly do not carry us far enough.

The trader's siding is, it may be, a mile or two away from the station, and the trader has daily, let us say, 10 tons of soap, or chocolate, for distribution all over England : these 10 tons may be going to 200 different destinations in consignments of 1 cwt. each. How is this contingency to be met ?

Probably they will require for satisfactory despatch and loading to be distributed among 30 or 40 wagons leaving the goods station for as many destinations for transhipment. The only satisfactory arrangements between the trader and the company will be the following alternatives :—

1. Load all goods in a tranship wagon from siding to the nearest station to be thence despatched. This would be a special service involving extra cost and entitling the railway to some special charge over and above the conveyance rate.
2. Load in wagons at the siding only consignments of such size as will secure a minimum load of 2 tons to destination, and cart the small packages to the station by road.
3. Recognise the railway tranship stations as legitimate points to which wagon loads of 2 tons may be loaded for transhipment and cart all other small consignments to station.

There are probably private sidings where an arrangement of the last-named description is in force, and traders will readily recognise the importance of the arrangement when the matter is explained, and the advantage of the arrangement to themselves. The particular arrangement to be chosen from the alternatives set out will, of course, depend upon the character of the traffic as well as the situation of the siding in relation to the forwarding station.

Consider the second alternative : to adopt it it may be necessary for the trader to hold back packages for certain stations or groups of stations to one or two specific days of the week (instead of despatching daily), so as to accumulate larger quantities for one place or district. This may not be practicable with all kinds of traffic, but it will with many.

It is clear, moreover, that this question needs different treatment in the case of a soap or chocolate factory from what it would be in the case of an ironworks or an agricultural implement factory.

Many traders are nowadays securing their own traffic despatch clerk—an official whose business it is to study railway methods with a view to obtaining for their own traffic the most effective handling and despatch whilst the traffic—received or forwarded—is in transit. The local railway agent should make it a point to explain thoroughly to the trader's despatch clerk the arrangements of the railway company, and by leaving with him a copy of the company's transhipping lists so that he may see the railway point of view, he can with a little education become by co-operation of great help in contributing to economical handling of his traffic and in obtaining the best services for the firm he represents.

The writer may here relate an incident that came within his own experience to show how practical this question of the education of traders is. A large firm in the Midlands doing business on a very extensive scale in consignments of 4 or 5 cwt. each, and which had got into the way of despatching their goods daily or almost every day, making up the load to just over one ton (in the days when that quantity was the stipulated minimum load for a through wagon). Not only were they indignant to a degree when they heard of the new proposals for transhipping all loads under 2 tons, but they gave violent expression to their "righteous wrath," and threatened diversion to a rival route of all their traffic.

A judicious inspector told off for the purpose called and explained to one of the principals of the firm the reason for the change and the full meaning of it ; whereupon the latter became sufficiently interested to set aside a day for personal inspection of the railway company's altered transhipping arrangements, the result of which was that the trader's representative was so pleased with the ingenuity of the altered general arrangements and satisfied that the new scheme was in the interests of the better despatch of traffic generally—his own included—that he took the railway instructions home and insisted on their being worked to at his own despatch siding, with advantage to his own goods and much economy in the use of railway trucks : his traffic in the future seldom being loaded out in less than 2-ton lots.

It is difficult for any trader at a fixed point of despatch to realise the intricacies of transit. Under a system in which a consignment of goods is held back for twenty-four hours so that there may be an aggregation of traffic in weight to justify a through wagon, as against a staging of the consignment by sections of its journey involving two or three transhipments, the sending trader will probably only see the *apparent* delay at his own end, and leave out of account the saving of one, two, or even three days which easily may be saved in course of transit by the avoidance of transhipment. These are the things that need to be brought home to the trader by careful explanation.

The type of wagon to be used for tranships is an important question, and experience has led to the adoption of the high-sided covered wagon for this purpose. A good standard wagon of this type is illustrated opposite page 120 (Fig. 13). It is "plated" to carry 12 tons with a tare weight of about 5¾ tons, and has side doors opening laterally on hinges on both sides. Nearly all companies have wagons of this description, though they vary in capacity and tare weight.

It is seldom that even as much as 8 tons can be packed into this wagon, as an average full load would not be more than 5 or 6 tons, the cubical capacity of the wagon fixing this limit. The actual load must depend very much upon the traffic of which the consignments consist. If it were well packed with consignments of imported bacon in cases, it might hold 8½ or 9 tons, or with slag or manure. It might even hold 10 or 12 tons of any of the following articles: alkali, barytes, bricks (packed), lead, sand, slates, sugar (in bags).

Other common articles whose bulk will not allow of such good loads as bacon or slag being secured are set out below with the weight of a filled wagon of the type referred to :—

	T.	C.
Hay and clover	2	13
Millboard	7	0
Sulphate of ammonia	7	10
Onions	6	0
Paper	7	6
Potatoes .. .. 3 tons 10 cwt. to 7 tons 10 cwt. according to packing.		
Slag wool	2	10
Sanitary tubes	4	0
Press-packed straw	3	0
Wool	3	15
Ale in barrels	4	4
Bran	5	10
Grease and tallow	6	0
Oranges	6	0
Peat moss	6	4
Carrots	5	15

Let us now consider the actual operation of the transhipping at a goods station. It is a complex operation, and the designing of a conveniently arranged building offers great opportunity for ingenuity. As a matter of fact, most of our transhipping in England is carried out at goods stations which were in no way designed originally for transhipping purposes.

In the lay-out of transhipping station buildings there are two vitally differing principles on which construction may be based, and in practice the different stations existing to-day are built on one or other of these lines or on a combination or adaptation of both. These distinctions are: (1) a tranship station pure and simple where the building and organisation is practically given up entirely to the unloading, sorting, and re-loading of tranships; or (2) a goods station at a large town where the traffic to and from the town in question is dealt with along with the tranship traffic. Under the former head are such tranship stations as Crewe, Gateshead, and others; under the second are most of the goods stations in London and at many of the large towns of the country. There is much to be said on behalf of each alternative, but the choice must be settled having regard to local circumstances.

The organisation of the staff at a tranship station is a matter on which the successful working of the whole station depends—it is one to which much attention has of late been given. At nearly all tranship stations the gang system is in operation, each wagon being loaded or unloaded by a "gang" of men. A gang will usually consist of a checker, loader, or "caller-off," and two, three, or four barrowmen. The loader (or "caller-off") unloads the goods, consignment by consignment, calling off each as it passes out of the wagon to the checker, who directs the barrowmen as to where it is to be taken for re-loading.

At Crewe every outward wagon (for its specific destination—Manchester, Leeds, York, Derby, or wherever it may be) has its appropriate berth allocated and numbered consecutively, so that the instructions to the barrowmen as a consignment for Leeds is unloaded is "No. 68," this indicating the Leeds wagon bench allocation.

At many tranship stations the bonus system of payment to the men has been put into operation. Under this system a normal quantity of goods is fixed as a day's work, say 50 tons for one gang to dispose of, loading or unloading as the case may be, and for every ton dealt with above this datum figure an additional amount is added to the normal daily wage. It would probably take the form of 9d. or 1s. for each extra ton above 50 handled per shift, to be divided amongst the men forming the gang.

The status of loader at a transhipping shed is important, but the question has been already enlarged upon in the chapters dealing with "Loaders and Loading" (Chapter VII) and "Organisation of a Goods Station" (Chapter X), and we need not now dilate further upon it.

We may, however, repeat what was said about the wages of the men: whereas a "gang," consisting of checker, loader, caller-off, and three porters, would before the war have been receiving as a week's wages in the aggregate (apart from bonus) probably about £7 8s., the standard wages in these post-war days will be checker 54s., loader and caller-off (each) 54s., three porters (each) 44s.—total £14 14s. We have here a very good illustration of how wages have been affected by the circumstances of war, and the bonus figure (stated above as a pre-war arrangement) will probably have been affected in similar degree.

I have tried in this chapter to explain what we mean in principle by transhipping: the application of the principle has to be worked out in its relation to the circumstances of each individual company; and the "Transhipping Instructions" of each railway company alone form a pamphlet of no inconsiderable size and of considerable importance. We may see something of the difference of circumstances between now and a quarter of a century ago. Then, in the absence of any co-ordinated system, a station such as, shall we say, Watford, with a package of goods for Kendal would send it to Crewe or Manchester, assuming as we may that the Watford goods agent's knowledge would carry him so far as to know that either of those stations was somewhere in the direction of Kendal, the destination. Crewe would then, when the package arrived, perhaps send the goods on to Carnforth or Preston, or to any place forward, towards Kendal, to which he might have a direct wagon going, and by unco-ordinated stages the package would get through. Now, however, the transhipping and road-van instructions are such that any forwarding station such as Watford can by reference to them determine in advance the right route and method of handling all consignments through to destination on each railway's system, the several companies exchanging their instructions between themselves. So that a station in Devon or Cornwall is expected to understand how to deal with a consignment of 5 cwt. for Wooler in Northumberland so as to secure for the goods the most economical and expeditious transit on its through journey.

We have mentioned road-vans—"roaders" they are sometimes called in the South of England—or "peddle cars" in the expressive language of our railway confrères on the other side of the Atlantic. These are the wagons which pick up and set down at the wayside stations on a branch line at each of which the goods traffic to be dealt with daily can be but small, and where a road-van is employed to work to and from a more important station to collect, in the case of forwarded traffic, the small consignments so as to work them into the more important streams of traffic out of which loads of a more favourable character can be obtained. These more important stations will usually be themselves sub-tranship stations ; and all the road-vans and the branch lines they work will themselves be listed, catalogued and classified in regard to the tranship stations to or from which they work ; and such road-van list will be circulated all over the country for the information of all officials throughout Great Britain who are themselves engaged in traffic working.

CHAPTER XII

A MARSHALLING YARD

ONE of the most important features upon any railway system as affecting the make-up of freight trains, and therefore the train load, is the marshalling yard. Just as the tranship station or shed was shown (in our last chapter) to have great importance in the obtaining of a good wagon load, so upon the proper organisation of the marshalling yard depends the good loading of the trains despatched therefrom. In Fig. 23 is given the daily number of wagons in one month leaving one of the busy yards in the North of England, and this statement will furnish a good foundation of fact on which to commence our consideration of the function of a marshalling yard. It will be seen that during the month 130,000 wagons left the yard (or about 5,000 every day), and all these wagons had to be shunted, or marshalled, in the yard, and made up into train loads to despatch to their varying destinations. These destinations may be North, South, East or West; and the size, or maximum loads, in each direction vary. The work of the yard-master and his staff is to marshal or classify the wagons for forward despatch in such a manner as will give the best operating results; in America the term applied is the "classification yard," because in the yard the wagons are classified according to their varying destinations and trains. It will be appreciated at once that the problem is a sufficiently intricate one, calling for a highly trained mind—or rather for the co-operation of a number of trained minds—to handle it.

Let us first direct our attention to a terminal despatch point in London from which there is a volume of work in the forwarding or despatching of wagons. The wagon loads for the various destinations have first to be considered, and the sidings are then allocated to the different destinations for which any considerable number of wagons are daily forwarded. The whole of the sidings in the yards are in this way scheduled for specific receiving points.

Manchester, Liverpool and Birmingham are important stations to which goods wagons in full trains are forwarded, and Crewe is another point to which tranship goods for various receiving points in the North of England are regularly forwarded from London.

As wagons for these places are loaded in the goods station or shed they will be shunted out into the yard and placed in the siding scheduled for their specific destination. Then when a train load is made up for destination the engine couples on at its booked or pre-arranged time, and the train starts away on its journey.

Having got a train load of wagons ready for Manchester or Crewe, the only thing is to couple on the engine and be off with the load. But when the destination is, say, for such a station as Leeds, where the load is destined for a variety of different places beyond, in such case it will most likely be found that the receiving company wishes to receive—or regards it as imperative that it should receive—the wagons in a certain order of arrangement, say the northern half of the system separate from those destined for the southern half. Or let us imagine that the wagons are for various wayside stations between Stafford and Crewe, and the train regulations require that the wagons should be marshalled in station order before they leave London. Either of these illustrations involves the operation of "second sorting" or "station-ordering"—a process of shunting which is subsidiary to the main marshalling involved in sorting out the wagons in the first instance into their respectively allocated sidings as a full train.

This second sorting operation is generally performed by means of a second sorting "grid" or group of short sidings arranged specifically for the purpose, and called "grid" because of its gridiron shape in design.

The principal sections or divisions of a marshalling yard are: (1) the reception sidings; (2) the marshalling sidings; (3) the grid or second sorting sidings; and (4) the departure sidings. And now having detailed these sections of the yard, it is necessary to have a diagram to refer to, and Fig. 24 illustrates the marshalling yard at Wath,

FIG. 23.—STATEMENT SHOWING NUMBER OF TRAINS AND NUMBER OF WAGONS LEAVING YARD A DURING MONTH OF JUNE 1907.

Date.	No. of Trains Leaving Yard.	No. of Wagons Attached in Yard.			Remarks.
		Loaded.	Empty.	Total.	
June 1	95	3,608	1,267	4,875	
2	82	3,555	1,104	4,659	
3	52	2,365	620	2,985	Sunday
4	61	2,073	859	2,932	
5	86	2,837	1,377	4,114	
6	98	3,768	1,260	5,028	
7	102	3,994	1,215	5,209	
8	102	3,790	1,308	5,098	
9	97	3,892	1,139	5,031	
10	47	2,287	472	2,759	Sunday
11	60	1,977	887	2,864	
12	91	3,002	1,231	4,233	
13	95	3,424	1,197	4,621	
14	102	3,923	1,448	5,371	
15	100	3,925	1,385	5,310	
16	95	3,962	1,261	5,223	
17	46	2,236	623	2,859	Sunday
18	57	1,861	786	2,647	
19	85	3,011	1,031	4,042	
20	103	3,430	1,391	4,821	
21	102	3,897	1,280	5,177	
22	102	3,944	1,158	5,102	
23	95	3,784	1,245	5,029	
24	46	2,155	586	2,741	Sunday
25	58	2,023	914	2,937	
26	94	3,201	1,187	4,388	
27	102	3,616	1,378	4,994	
28	97	3,721	1,243	4,964	
29	102	3,674	1,460	5,134	
30	93	3,480	1,236	4,716	
Total ..	2,547	96,415	33,448	129,863	

(*Signed*)...............

Yard-Master.

worked on the gravity system, and one of the best equipped in the country.

We have referred to a terminal despatch yard, but a typical marshalling yard is not terminal; it is intermediate between train working on either side of it and dealing with both up and down traffic as in the case of the Wath yard.

There are three main variations of the principle in the construction of marshalling yards—the flat shunting yard, the gravity (or gravitation) yard, and the hump shunting yard.

We shall refer to each in turn, but we proceed to describe a yard worked on the gravity system (see Fig. 24).

A train arrives with a miscellaneous collection of wagons for various destinations. It first seeks repose in one of the reception sidings until the convenient hour arrives for it to be put over the hump or highest point of the yard, which is generally at or near to a signal cabin or frame wherein dwells the signalman or pointsman in control of the operations. As wagon by wagon passes over a summit at point F on the diagram it runs down by gravity into its appropriate siding according to destination, in the group of classification sidings marked "westbound traffic" on the diagram—the main group of sidings shown in the diagram. The method of up-to-date control and operation is as follows :—

The group of marshalling sidings of which there are 30—15 on each side of the centre through running lines known as the "switch street"—are numbered with odd numbers on one side from 1 to 29 ; on the other with the even numbers 2 to 30 ; and are controlled by switch points (facing points), each operated by a piston lever set in motion by electric current from the cabin, so that the signalman by a simple electric push can set the points for any siding number required. As the wagons at the summit are released in consecutive "cuts" by a shunter they are all marked in chalk on the buffer beam with the number of siding they are destined for, and this acts as the indication to the signalman in the box as to the siding points he is to set. The points being rightly set and the wagon or "cut" of two or three wagons being on their way down the gravity sidings, the only thing remaining to do is to steady the wagons to rest as they run down under their own momentum ; and this is the main business of the shunting yard, for which a posse of shunters are provided. Their function is to catch the wagons in motion, put on the brakes so as to check the speed, and afterwards regulate the speed by applying leverage to the brake handles just so as to allow the wagons to run to the point where they should come to rest in the siding they are destined for. It is a delicate operation, and one in which some considerable exercise is necessary to "make perfect."

The wagons having collected in their various sidings, duly sorted in accordance with their ultimate destination, are transferred as a made up train to the departure sidings, where a van is attached, and the engine comes on and takes hold of the train for departure at the pre-determined or booked departure time.

Where the system of train-loading cards is adopted, these cards are collected by a boy told off for the purpose as the train is in the departure siding, and handed to the guard, who thereby receives his card index of the tare and contents weight of each wagon in his custody.

There is usually an inspector or a foreman in supervision of the departure siding who is responsible for the whole of the work done in the siding. It is his duty to see that the operations are expeditiously and satisfactorily performed and that trains are despatched at their booked time.

As samples of a good gravitation yard may be mentioned Wath (G.C.); Feltham (L. & S.W.); Edge Hill, Liverpool (L. & N.W.); Shildon (N.E.R. Mineral); Edge Hill is well equipped with second sorting "grids," which are absent from Wath. Wath, on the other hand, is a duplicated yard, having separate areas for "up" and "down," or rather for east-going and west-going traffic, these two sections being a replica the one of the other.

To give some idea of the staff required at a yard of this magnitude, Wath—through which pass on the average about 130,000 wagons per month—we may give the following list applicable to each of the two yards:—

Three head shunters, twelve shunters, three signalmen and three inspectors: the multiples of three indicating that the yard is always at work day and night (twenty-four hours) and the three men work round the twenty-four hours.

In a gravity yard like Wath the work of propelling is done by the natural force of gravity, and the work of the shunters is, as above explained, almost entirely confined to braking the wagons down the inclines ; they are really brakesmen, but they retain the name of the grade originally fixed for the men who control the shunting of wagons in a "flat" yard.

If, as in the case of Wath, the yard is in close proximity to the collieries, the yard-master will probably be much in requisition to look after the colliery working. The working of any colliery is greatly dependent upon its getting a regular supply of coal empties (for if empty wagons are not available, with most collieries a stoppage of the coal output is occasioned), and the supply and allocation of coal empties is very largely a matter resting with the yard-master. In times of wagon shortage this official is kept busy at his end of the telephone system by the exigent demands of impatient and importunate coalowners.

Having spoken of a gravitation yard, we may now describe a flat shunting yard. The diagram used to illustrate the gravity yard with its summit cabin will equally illustrate a yard on the level, if it be remembered that there is no summit or hump, but that the ground is on the level. It is in the method of working the yard where the difference occurs. There will probably be no signal cabin, but the various points will be worked by tumbler or "dummy" levers on the ground fixed at the point where each "switch" leads off. The shunters' function differs from that of the shunters in gravity yards, inasmuch as in the flat yard their important duty is to alter the points for the sets of wagons as they are propelled forward by the locomotive, and to pin the brakes on when the wagon comes to rest. It is not, as in the case of a gravity yard, the main business to brake or control the wagons which are running under momentum of their own, but the chief aim and object is to get the wagons forward, which can only be accomplished by steady propulsion from the locomotive. This means, as reference to the diagram shows at once, that the engine has to perform a protracted series of backward and forward movements corresponding exactly to the number of cuts into which the wagons have to be broken up. It is true that a somewhat less powerful engine can perform the same amount of work as a heavier type which has to push over a summit, but it takes a considerably longer time necessarily. Therefore, to deal with the same number of wagons in a given time as could be dealt with in a gravity yard, more engine time is necessary, and every hour of engine time curtailed represents a very considerable economy in cost in engine shunting. The engines used in the Wath gravitation yard are very powerful ones built for the purpose (they are of the 0–6–4 type), and the writer has himself seen (January 10, 1919) a mixed train of 74 wagons put over the summit with 21 " cuts " in 14 minutes, averaging 40 seconds for each " cut," to run down into its siding and make way for the next. I believe several minutes would be necessary for each cut on the level—a difference of great importance in a shunting yard where at certain times of day great aggregations of traffic take place and where congestion occurs at once if things are not kept moving.

As to " hump shunting " marshalling yards, there is not much to be said beyond that this method is a sort of hybrid arrangement, and takes a place between the gravitation yard and the flat or level yard. Where natural gradients can be found which lend themselves to the construction of a gravitation yard the question largely settles itself, but there are many cases where the cost of a complete gravity yard being prohibitive, it is yet found abundantly worth while to make an artificial hump over which a train is shunted, and the natural force of gravity is assisted by locomotive power just as much as may be found necessary. Many marshalling yards in level country have found it desirable to construct a hump for shunting purposes for the main group of sorting sidings.

The question of the general design of a shunting yard is too complex and technical to deal with in a treatise such as this. The standard will necessarily have to be modified according to local physical circumstances. The arrangement of " up " and " down " yards in relation to each other, the nature of the ground (level or undulating), the " run round " lines for the engines, the provision of hospital (damaged wagon) sidings, the site of the van sidings, and other considerations afford great scope for the ingenuity of the traffic engineer, especially when all these problems have to be solved within limits rigorously fixed by the location of approach lines, which often come from several directions at the same time.

One general comment should here be made in regard to our British marshalling yards: they have nearly all of them grown with the growth of traffic, and often present the appearance of old and much patched garments. Like "Topsy," they've "just growed," having been added to from time to time as traffic has required. Planned originally, therefore, for a comparatively small traffic, in many cases they are not laid out in such a way as to provide for the most economical method for handling the large traffic that now passes through them.

Some of the yards of a local character which deal mostly with the traffic of a restricted area are generally laid out to serve their required ends, and there are a few—very few—well-designed modern yards: some we have referred to. But the marshalling points for the main highways of traffic need to be afresh determined, and especially now that the railway companies are working together as a united and co-operative system. The yards at Crewe and at Wath (in South Yorkshire) are in good strategic positions, but the traffic working conditions which may arise as the result of grouping of the railways will no doubt lead to consideration of other strategic points being selected, and the probability is that new marshalling yards will before long be planned and provided so as to give the most economical facilities for the shunting of the traffic.

The difficulty which has hitherto existed has arisen largely from the competitive system under which we have been living. An improved shunting or classification yard will always serve to benefit the train working all round, and very often it may benefit other railway systems even more than the railway company on whose system it is constructed. It could hardly be expected that company "A" would construct at its own cost an elaborate marshalling yard or transhipping station if, say, one-third, or it might be one-half, of the economy or saving to be reaped from such construction was to go to the benefit of companies "B" and "C." But the new *régime* of railway grouping now being entered upon will give opportunity for marshalling yards to be designed at various points in the country where they can most economically deal with the traffic of the country as a whole, and the appropriation of such financial savings as may result would have to be fixed by inter-company agreement. Clearly, the exact determination of these yards both as to internal design and the best *locus in quo* would require much united co-operative thought, but it should be possible now to plot down on a map of England some territorial division which would enable the most advantageous strategic positions to be adopted for the marshalling yards of the future.

It now only remains to say something about the personnel of the yard. I have left this matter to the last, for it is really the most important of all. First of all we must speak of the yard-master. But what is a yard-master? The term is a comparatively new one in this connection, and whilst "yard-master" may have come as a term from the West, the latter part of it comes with forceful and very ancient but honourable meaning from the East, and needs to be re-established in its true and pristine nobility of the word. We must have masters in the right sense—not masters in distinction or contra-distinction to "men," but masters who in the highest sense *are* men by virtue of their being masters of their work. It is more than ever important in these days of mechanical work, when steam and electric power are directing the general setting of our lives increasingly towards a mechanical environment, that we determine we will be masters of our lives, of our fate, of the great machine in which we are being more and more engulfed. For we must realise that if we cannot master our fate and our environment, and the machines we play or work with, they will very soon become master of us. Is not the great art of life in these days to keep oneself from drifting into a conventional or mechanical habit of living, which we can only do by preserving our personality? Personality must control mechanics.

The qualifications necessary for a good yard-master are manifold: he must be a man of great mental aptitude; he must have a keen intellect, with a natural fondness for figures and complex problems, for he requires to take a daily survey of the yard with statistical figures, and to understand their meaning. He must know the relative advantages of the various kinds of wagons in use on his railway, and a sufficient knowledge of the points of a locomotive and their relative capacities to enable him to arrange engine distribution intelligently and economically; he must have a good knowledge of the geography, not only of the line upon which he is employed, but of other railways, and a great faith in the possibility of improvements. Above all, he must have faith in humanity—of the human units around him, and a knowledge that they will respond to kindly treatment; in other words, he must have a tactful method of dealing with his staff, and so of obtaining from them a maximum amount of effort. To quote an American writer: "His work is movement, his danger is blockade. When we think of the enormous number of complicated vehicles with their various consignments coming in regular flow by thousands into the marshalling yard, the yard-master needs to be something more than a 'parcels handler.' A good yard should be kept in good condition if it is to do the work required of it. A complicated yard means a blocked road—an absolutely useless and expensive tool; and a block in the marshalling yard may easily be brought about any day, not by doing the wrong thing, but simply by not doing enough of the right. In times of emergency it is not the right policy of the yard-master, as it is in so many other cases, to watch and wait. Delay is often fatal. The yard-master must do something vigorously, even if it be far from the best thing, and he must keep on going without admitting for a moment an impossibility. The ideal man for this post ought to have an aptitude for meeting small and great emergencies quite beyond the simple ability to follow rules. He must be resourceful."

So far as the marshalling yard is concerned, the yard-master's next-in-charge is the foreman or inspector. In a composite yard there will be a foreman in charge of each section; and over each sub-section, if this grouping is applicable, there would be a head shunter or charge shunter with his gang of under shunters and assistant shunters or brakesmen. As has been already pointed out, the actual nomen-

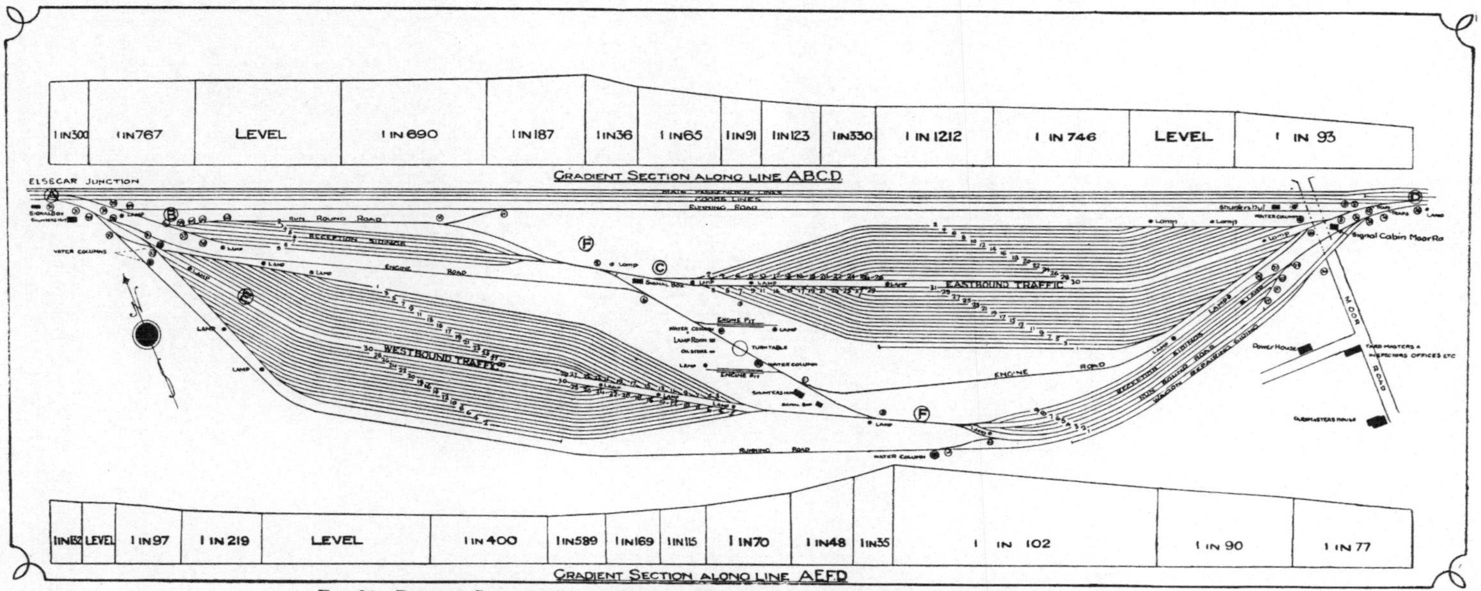

Fig. 24.—Diagram Showing Arrangement of Marshalling Sidings; Gravity Yard at Wath, G.C.R.

clature of grades will depend somewhat upon the physical character and lay-out of the yard.

But the great secret of success in a marshalling yard, as in a goods or transhipping station, or any place where there is a large aggregation of traffic, is hearty and genuine co-operation between all grades at work in the yard: by each man knowing his own work and what is expected of him, and contributing of his best as to a great service in which he knows his own work is necessary for real success. In introducing and maintaining this right spirit of service and a healthy co-operative *esprit de corps* the influence of the yard-master is all-important.

Very much has been done of recent years towards making more safe the conditions under which the men have to work in these yards, and no considerations of the heavy cost involved ought to stand in the way of such improvements of facilities as the following:—

1. The best possible system of lighting a marshalling yard.
2. All point levers should be whitewashed so as to be visible at night-time.
3. Point rodding should be boxed in whenever possible.

I have referred to the yard-master taking a statistical survey of his yard. He should have before him every day the aggregate number of wagons dealt with on the preceding day, and this figure should be tabulated so as to give a statistical survey. When a record number of wagons is obtained, the fact should be widely made known, for it encourages a spirit of emulation. This is best and most satisfactorily done by the publication of a tabulated record at the yard-master's or yard-foreman's office. I have been told that this is useless, that men do not care about these figures and will not look at them. This I do not believe, personally. It *may be* that only two or three out of a dozen would be interested in knowing when records are broken in regard to wagons dealt with in their own yard, but such two or three are the keen and intelligent ones in the yard. Keenness is contagious, and others become affected in time ; and it is more than worth any trouble that may be involved in preparing and posting the figures, if only to stimulate the interest and curiosity of a comparatively small but intelligent section of the men.

For the yard-master's own information and consideration he should have before him :—

1. Number of wagons entering and/or departing from the yard daily.
2. Number of trains entering and/or departing from the yard daily.
3. Shunting engine-hours employed in the yard (divided between train engines and shunting engines).
4. Wagons entering yard per hour, per engine shunting hour, and per man hour of shunting staff.
5. Wages paid to yard staff : (*a*) per wagon entering ; (*b*) per engine hour.
6. Cost per wagon for engine shunting.
7. Time spent in the yard per train (applicable only to yards where most of the trains enter the yard and again proceed on their journey).

The statistical figures of a marshalling yard will again be referred to in the next chapter dealing with " Statistical Control," but I append hereto a statistical summary of the work in one of our marshalling yards.

The reduced amount of work per hour which by this return appears to be the general result in the yard is probably not in any way due to inefficiency or slackness on the part of those responsible for the yard work, but more likely to the yard itself already in 1912 being taxed to its full capacity for handling wagons ; and whenever we attempt, either with a locomotive or with station and fixed accommodation, to make the machine or accommodation do more than its capacity at the time of construction was intended to deal with, we shall inevitably get poor and declining results. I give the statement, not because of the story it tells, but as a sample of the general form in which it is possible to get the work of any given yard summarised and reflected statistically.

SUMMARY FIGURES OF A SPECIFIC MARSHALLING YARD.

Year.	Number of Wagons Entering Yard.		Yard Wages per Wagon Entering.	Pilot Working Average No. of Wagons Shunted per Hour.		Remarks.
	Total.	Per Engine Hour.	Pence.	Up Side.	Down Side.	
1912	671,198	28·57	0·71	42	57	National Strike of Miners, March
1913	764,735	28·35	0·71	43	59	
1914	724,653	27·23	0·83	41	55	War Period
1915	699,590	25·41	0·95	37	53	War Period
1916	701,276	24·26	1·09	37	53	War Period
1917	681,006	23·82	1·24	39	55	War Period

The Ministry of Transport are now being supplied with information regarding selected marshalling yards showing—

Number of trains entering, and
Number of wagons detached :—
- Loaded.
- Empty.
- Total.

Number of trains departing.
Engine shunting hours :—
- Train engines.
- Shunting engines.
- Total.

Number of wagons detached :—
- Per total engine hour.
- Per working day.
- Per train.

Hours on duty of shunting staff.
Number of wagons detached per man hour on duty of shunting staff.
Total wages paid to shunting staff.
Number of wagons detached per £ of wages paid.

From these figures compiled by the various companies many useful statistical tests may be adopted.

CHAPTER XIII

STATISTICS AS A FACTOR IN FREIGHT TRAIN OPERATING

We have at various times throughout these chapters referred to statistical units, as for instance in the chapter on train loads, when we compared the average train load, firstly one year with another, and secondly with the actual and maximum results in daily working; or again, when in Chapter XII on the marshalling yard we spoke of the units, (1) wagons dealt with per engine hour, and (2) yard wages per wagon entering the yard, by means of which we may compare the working results period by period or one yard with another.

It is, however, essential that in any such statistical comparision of results a knowledge of the circumstances of the marshalling yards under review be possessed before any useful criticism can be made, and in measuring the work done by these units regard must also be paid to:—

(1) The difference in the lay-out of the yards, this factor involving considerably more shunting at some yards than at others.

(2) Density of the traffic in the different districts, particularly when comparing the results of one yard with another; and fluctuation in traffic, as it is not always possible to reduce expenses commensurate with the falling off in the amount of traffic dealt with.

In any marshalling yard, at any station, or in any operating department of a railway, it may be taken for granted that there will always be a certain number of persons who are intelligently interested in statistical comparisons, and it will be found that the publication or the possession of statistical information is in itself a stimulus to improved working; for the discussion of the facts which the figures reveal and the endeavour to understand the meaning of the differences and of the causes which account for these differences will often be found to suggest alterations in practical working, as the meaning of the differences is brought home to those who can alter or affect the working conditions: for the natural and instinctive desire in the human heart to excel or to achieve improving results is one of the main driving forces which affect or determine the course of industry.

But the first and most important stage as a precedent to altered action is that the meaning of the figures under consideration be understood, and it may be stated as a general proposition at the outset that the meaning of statistical figures is not always easy of understanding. Often the true meaning is hidden: the figures need study, and any attempt to judge of them superficially or to make use of them before their meaning is grasped only leads astray. And figures alone, without the necessary understanding of the units they refer to, or it may be the relationship which they bear to others, are of no practical value.

The following table illustrates how easily one may be led astray by an improper or inadequate presentation of statistical information. It represents five years of train working (goods and mineral trains) on a supposititious railway system, and records the number of trains worked in a district with their average loads.

Number of Goods and Mineral Trains with Their Average Loads of Freight—First Week in December.

Years 1917 *to* 1921, *P.Q.R. Railway.*

Year.	Total Freight Trains Worked.		Analysis of Trains and Loads as Between			
			Goods Trains.		Mineral Trains.	
	No. of Trains.	Average Load in Tons.	No. of Trains.	Average Load in Tons.	No. of Trains.	Average Load in Tons.
1917	32	257·4	13	123	19	350
1918	35	251·3	15	125	20	346
1919	37	257·5	16	123	21	360
1920	39	261·0	14	120	25	340
1921	45	263·0	15	117	30	336

Let us examine the above table. If we do not scrutinise it beyond the first, i.e. the total, column, we appear to see steady progress: the number of trains shows a gradual increase, and—since the year 1917 at any rate—the average load seems to have been steadily increasing. Indeed, the average load of all the trains has increased year by year. But examination of the remaining columns shows that the whole reason is found in the increasing number of mineral trains which has sent up the average load of the whole number of trains, *although the average size in tons of both the goods trains and the mineral trains separately has declined.* A table which presents the aggregate figures only conceals the decrease in train loads and shows an apparent steady increase in the loads of freight trains worked.

The great danger in the handling of statistics by the non-expert is that of adding together as of equal value things that are quite different and treating them all as equal, adding cows to elephants or lilies to roses, etc. It is the mistake of concluding that a man with six sixpences and six shillings in his pockets is a richer man than another who has ten half-crowns, because the former has twelve separate pieces of money. A mineral train is entirely different from a goods train, and worked under quite different circumstances, and the two should not be added together unless the requirements warrant it.

This danger is perhaps brought out more clearly if we take the sales of some simple commodity. Take for example a seller of bulbs. Assume that in three successive weeks he sells two kinds of bulbs of lesser and greater value: of the lesser (let us say snowdrops) he sells successively 50, 60, and 80, but at a reducing price, say $1\frac{1}{2}$d., $1\frac{1}{4}$d., and 1d. respectively. Of the better bulbs (tulips, it may be) he sells also an increasing number, 50, 100, and 224 respectively, in the same period, at falling prices of 2s., 1s. 10d., and 1s. 9d. week by week. The average of all the bulbs sold would be respectively 1s. $0\frac{3}{4}$d., 1s. $2\frac{1}{4}$d. and 1s. $3\frac{3}{4}$d.; but though it may be some consolation for the all-round fall in prices to have sold an increasing number of the higher-priced bulbs, the salesman can hardly congratulate himself upon the improving price of his bulbs though the average price of bulbs sold in the aggregate as set out in the table below *appears* to have gone up:—

Bulbs Sold Each of the Three Weeks.	Snowdrops.		Tulips.		Total Bulbs Sold.	
	No.	Average Price.	No.	Average Price.	No.	Average Price.
		d.		s. d.		s. d.
First week	50	1½	50	2 0	100	1 0¾
Second week	60	1¼	100	1 10	160	1 2¼
Third week	80	1	224	1 9	304	1 3¾

So far, then, as regards the question, How statistics should *not* be used? or how figures may be made to mislead? Let us now deal with the constructive side, and try to bring out how, when properly selected and intelligently presented, statistics will illuminate.

Since the Ministry of Transport published the amended and additional railway statistics at the beginning of 1921 various units of measurement and comparison have been available which were not hitherto known in Great Britain, therefore this publication marks a conspicuous stage forward in the period of reconstruction after the war, and is one of the most hopeful factors for development. These statistics include, amongst many other units, those of ton miles on each great railway system, the average load of a freight wagon and of a freight train, and the average distance each ton of traffic was conveyed.[1] These and the average ton miles worked per train engine are selected as amongst the most important of the statistical units now published, and are set out for the principal English railway companies. The tables on the following page give the figures showing the factors named for the principal railway companies.

The true significance of these figures can only be appreciated by careful study. It is somewhat remarkable that it is only now for the first time, when for nearly a century we have been enjoying the advantages of railway transit, that the railway companies or the public at large have

[1] I am not dealing herein at all with passenger traffic, in respect of which also new figures are available.

known either the average load of a train or the average length of journey appertaining to the several lines. Some fourteen or fifteen years ago the North Eastern Railway published figures which showed that the average distance every ton of traffic was hauled on their railway was

YEAR 1920.

Company.	Net Ton Miles Aggregate in January.	Average Freight Train Load.	Average Distance Hauled.
Great Central	95,438,434	174·15	35·94
Great Eastern	59,649,384	102·58	53·30
Great Northern	94,937,859	156·36	45·89
Great Western	229,944,005	143·43	48·76
Lancashire and Yorkshire	52,571,948	139·01	25·36
L. & N.W.	198,912,652	140·35	43·55
Midland	257,221,359	145·11	54·11
North Eastern	160,501,428	154·81	32·25

24 miles, and Sir George Paish, writing in 1902 in his book entitled *The British Railway Position*, treating of the L. & N.W. Railway Company, assumed, with the knowledge of the N.E.R. figures, that an average haulage distance on the L. & N.W. Railway for their goods traffic was 34·8 miles. How far this estimate was from the actual facts of to-day as revealed above can be seen from the last column in the table. Yet this has been the best estimate hitherto available.

We repeat below the average load conveyed per wagon as previously set out in the chapter upon "The Wagon Load," so far as the principal railway companies are concerned. The figures are for April 1922 :—

Name of Railway Company.	Average Loads Per Wagon.	
	Coal Traffic. Tons.	All Freight Traffic, including Coal. Tons.
Great Central	8·8	6·24
Great Northern	8·4	5·4
Great Western	8·5	6·0
L. & N.W. (Northern)	8·0	4·6
L. & N.W. (Southern)	8·7	4·9
Midland	8·2	5·8
North Eastern	9·27	6·34
All companies	8·37	5·50

The above figures are true averages accurately calculated and obtained by dividing the aggregate wagon miles into the net aggregate ton miles of traffic.

Now let us set out the figures of TON MILES PER TRAIN ENGINE HOUR as it appears in the Ministry of Transport statistics, illustrating with the 1921 figures and taking the seven principal railway systems above selected.

The figures show as follows :—

Railway Company. Year 1921.	Ton Miles per	
	Total Engine Hour.	Train Engine Hour.
Great Central	404·91	867·27
Great Northern	527·50	989·21
Great Western	437·95	965·07
L. & N.W. (Northern)	262·60	697·17
L. & N.W. (Southern)	446·66	910·33
Midland	490·13	885·79
North-Eastern	452·46	1200·73
All companies	412·93	900·57

The volume of statistics now available published by the Ministry represents a very complex array of figures, and can be turned to a great variety of uses. The general manager's requirements in the way of figures is quite different from the requirement of the station master or (say) the wagon loader. And the use which would be made of the statistics by the railway companies' agents is entirely different from the use which an outside critic—a trader or a shareholder—would wish to make of them.

We must look at the statistics alternatively from the point of view of the general manager of the railway, that of the superintendent or other chief officer of the company, that of the station or yard master, and that of the wagon loader.

The figures taken for illustration of ton miles per engine or per train hour represent one of the most comprehensive of all the units which are included in the tables of figures now published. It is a very complex unit, for in reflecting as it does the aggregate amount of transport work, the movement of certain weight over a fixed distance in a given unit of time, viz. one hour, it practically takes into account the aggregate result of all delays, of good or bad loading, of accident, and all other factors which affect the movement of trains and wagons. One thousand ton miles per engine hour signifies a train load of 100 tons of traffic moved over 10 miles, or 10 tons of traffic moved 100 miles on the average in one hour.

There are two ways in which the engine hours can be computed : the amount of time occupied by engines shunting as apart from train working may be included, or it may not. It is manifest if we divide the transport result in ton miles over all the hours occupied by engines, whether working trains *or shunting in the various goods yards,* instead of simply over the hours of *engines working trains* on the running lines, the quantity of ton miles operated will be much smaller. The difference is shown in the two columns of the table on page 193.

This unit or factor of comparison, the ton miles per engine hour, is essentially a general manager's figure, for it gives in a comprehensive average the net operating results over the whole of his railway ; but it tells no story *in detail.*

A comparison of such a figure as " ton miles per engine hour " is of greater value when applied by one company statistically over a series of years than in comparison between company and company where circumstances are so different.

In 1908, before the parliamentary committee on Railway Accounts and Statistical Returns, the N.E.R. Company presented tables of the ton miles per engine hour on their system between 1902 and 1907, and the figures then given, which showed a very gratifying record of progress, have become of greater interest now that it is possible to add figures of a later date. The figures are given in the table opposite, brought up to date by the addition of corresponding figures between 1908 and 1911, and the figures for 1921 as published by the Ministry of Transport.

It will be noticed from the figures that the ton miles—the weight of traffic moved over distance definitely measured in the ton-mile unit—" operated " each train hour the locomotives were at work with trains had rather more than doubled during the period between 1902 and 1921. This is a very good illustration of the value of a statistical survey.

North Eastern Railway.

Year.	Ton Miles per Engine Hour.		
	Per Train Hour.	Per Shunting Hour.	Per Total Engine Hour.
	Freight.	Freight.	Freight.
1902	595	489	269
1903	652	511	287
1904	713	518	300
1905	762	542	317
1906	765	560	323
1907	751	571	324
1908	790	561	328
1909	855	597	351
1910	880	611	361
1911	870	597	354
*	*	*	*
1921	1201	726	452

When there is such a possibility of continuous development in this direction, the ton miles per engine hour ought to show a continuous upward line (as represented in the graph on page 196), and one is tempted to reflect that as long as this barometric indication is steadily upward, a general manager may feel satisfied with the general administration of the operating department, and may be *content to watch* so far as internal train working is concerned; but that when this barometer of "operating" results begins to fall he, the general manager, may be expected to become critical, or at least interrogative, as to the reasons of the fall.

Passing on to the chief officers of the company in the next rank, the figures used by the general manager as indications of traffic or working results will have a much more vivid and intensive significance to the goods manager or to the superintendent. In the minds of these officers the actual conditions affecting the figures are much more deeply

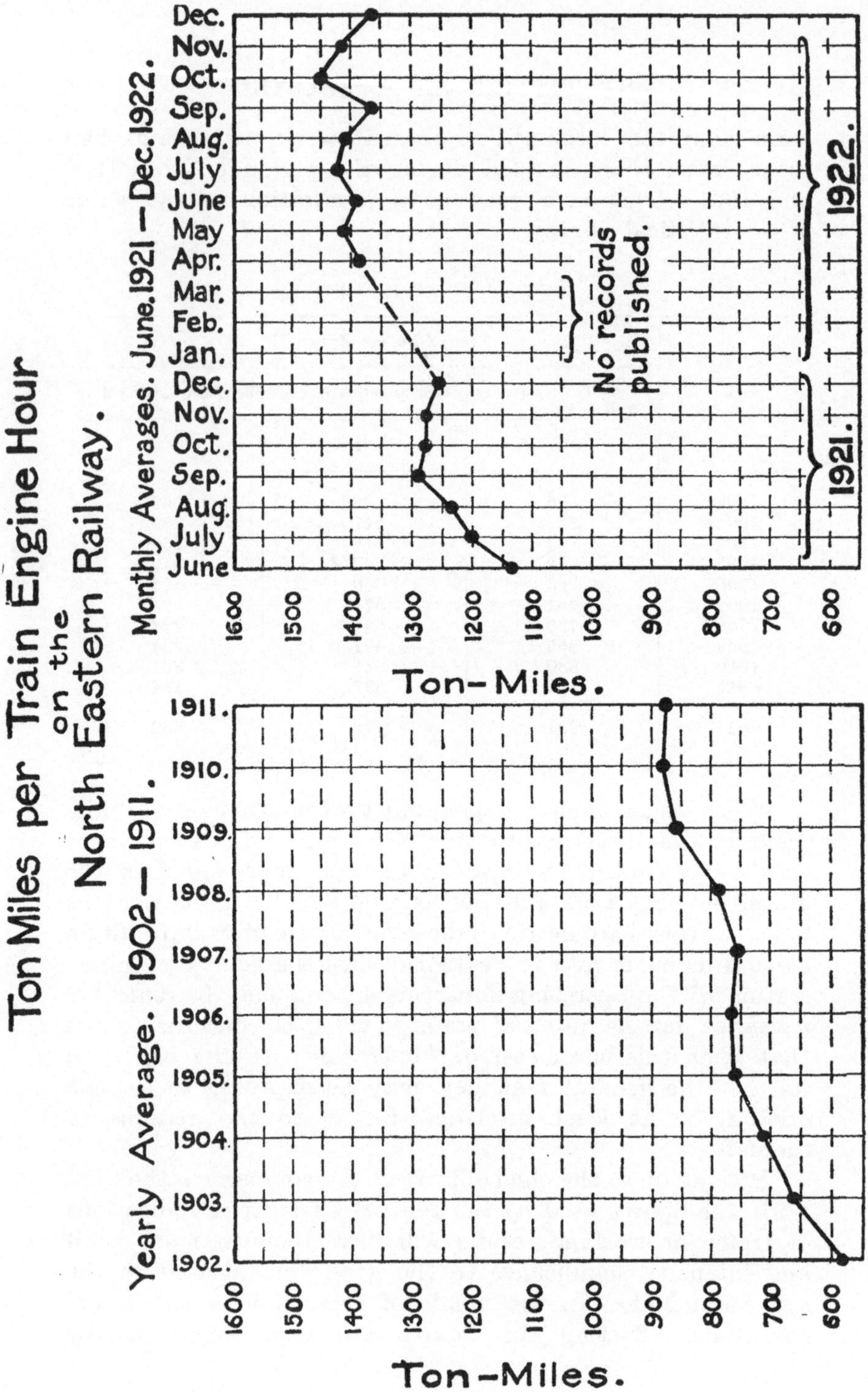
Ton Miles per Train Engine Hour on the North Eastern Railway.
Monthly Averages. June.1921 – Dec.1922.
June
July
Aug.
Sep.
Oct.
Nov.
Dec.
Jan.
Feb.
Mar.
Apr.
May
June
July
Aug.
Sep.
Oct.
Nov.
Dec.
No records published.
1921.
1922.
1600
1500
1400
1300
1200
1100
1000
900
800
700
600
Ton-Miles.
Yearly Average. 1902 – 1911.
1902.
1903.
1904.
1905.
1906.
1907.
1908.
1909.
1910.
1911.
1600
1500
1400
1300
1200
1100
1000
900
800
700
600
Ton-Miles.

Fig. 25.

engraved, and they immediately proceed to split up the figures into different districts or into varying traffics. A considerable breaking up or analysis of factors takes place with them, and a departmental officer will wish to use the figures of train loads split up into districts, loads of wagons, speed of trains, special causes of detention such as delay in working, proportion of empty wagon mileage, and many other factors on which statistical information is available. It is the business of the general superintendent to examine the facts of all these circumstances reflected in the figures, for he is responsible for seeing that the movement of the traffic is economically and efficiently carried out.

Then as we pass from the chief officers' point of view to that of the individual station master, goods agent, or their assistants on the spot, we may very shortly indicate the statistical units which will be of vital interest to these officials. These we have to some extent dealt with in preceding chapters, but we may summarise them here. In regard to the loading of wagons at specific stations, the station master or agent will watch carefully—(1) the tons loaded per wagon at each station month by month and day by day, (2) the wages cost per ton handled, (3) the number and percentage of empty wagons forwarded from his own station and from adjacent and similarly circumstanced stations which may have any appropriate comparison with his own.

The yard-master or inspector in charge of a local area of train working will want to know—(1) the total number of wagons or tons forwarded from his station area, as compared with former periods of comparison; (2) how his trains despatched were loaded as regards number of wagons; (3) were the wagons individually well loaded so as to contribute to a good average; (4) average train miles per engine hour worked in the area under review or in specific sections of it.

It will probably be found that one of the most effective ways of dealing with the periodical figures issued from the statistics office will be the arrangement of a meeting of all who are practically concerned with loading or working results to consider the figures affecting a particular district.

This will fall naturally upon the superintendent of the district to arrange. When he is assisted at such meeting by several yard-masters or inspectors and some of his principal station masters in the district, it is certain that the exchange of the information and the narration of each other's experience in regard to methods adopted for load improvement, and in regard to the description of wagon best adapted for particular traffics, will lead to a considerable improvement in mental equipment of every officer who has been present. Such meetings are of real educational value, and it is on many railway systems a regular practice to hold such gatherings periodically, at three or six months' intervals, or even more frequently.

Of the unit of average miles travelled by a ton of goods, the average haul, or average lead, as it is alternatively called, much might be said. From the commercial or rate-making point of view it has a special value, but this volume is hardly the place to treat of it in this connection. The importance of it will be seen the more when a series of years' comparisons can be given. From the *operating point of view*, it may be taken as a general principle that the longer the average haul of goods the greater is the opportunity for economical working; and it follows therefore that anything that can be done to increase the factor of average haul from year to year tends to an economy of working.

I have by no means detailed all the statistical factors which local officers will desire to bring into use; they are necessarily various, and each set of officers will best determine for themselves the figures most suited to their specific needs.

We may refer to a few more general considerations and facts bearing on the application of statistics. One of the chief facts that are brought out, and which the statistics record, is the extent of improvement in train loading which has in recent years been effected; and as far as we have information, this applies to all countries where there has been any extent of railway development. It is pre-eminently the case in America, where we find the statistics most complete, and we shall refer to this before we conclude. As regards England, we only have over a series of years the figures published by the North Eastern Railway as direct evidence of what has been accomplished in this way; and whether the results chronicled by that company may be taken as typical of a movement which has been general over the railways of Great Britain as a whole or not (and we believe they may), the figures are full of significance. The figures of train miles in hauling goods traffic on the North Eastern Railway are given below: they were, until all figures of this kind were suspended by the exigencies of war, annually published in Board of Trade returns.

After what has been said in previous chapters, it will be generally understood that the improved loading of every train conveying goods traffic soon makes its improvement felt in the reduction of the number of trains necessary for the same amount of traffic.

North Eastern Railway.

Year.	Miles Run by Freight Trains.
1890	15,191,900
1892	14,098,300
1894	15,642,900
1896	15,640,600
1898	16,800,100
1900	17,588,700
1902	14,932,800
1904	12,216,700
1906	12,338,300
1908	11,861,200
1910	11,326,300
1912	11,074,700

As the size (measured in weight of freight carried) of each train has grown, so also the receipts per train mile must have increased, and this is confirmed by the steady increase in the receipts per freight train mile shown also in the Board of Trade returns, and which are set out for three comparative years in the next following table.

It will be remembered that there are other factors affecting receipts as well as the mere loading of a train, as for instance any considerable change in the character of the traffic making up a train, but the general story told by these figures is unmistakable. There was no general revision of conveyance rates during the period here dealt with.

RECEIPTS PER TRAIN MILE ON THE FIVE UNDERMENTIONED COMPANIES, 1900–1906–1912.

Railway Company.	1900.	1906.	1912.
	s. d.	s. d.	s. d.
Great Western	4 11·1	6 6·7	7 7·2
Lancashire and Yorkshire ..	9 1·3	12 2·5	13 8·9
London and North Western ..	6 9·1	8 10·2	10 10·5
Midland	5 3·72	6 1·0	6 11·2
North Eastern	6 10·3	10 5·7	12 5·8

With such a distinct improvement as these figures appear to show, one is not surprised that a question is at once raised by those who are critical of railway management and whose main criterion as to the effectiveness thereof is in the annual declaration of the shareholders' dividend to the following effect. If such satisfactory results have been achieved, where are they shown in the accounts and financial returns of the companies in reduction of working cost? We can, so far as the North Eastern Company is concerned at least, find a pretty effective and satisfactory answer to this question. We would observe generally that in these days of rapidly expanding prices and continuous increase in wages and in the size of the staff of a big concern necessary to maintain it in a satisfactory working condition, that savings when made are rapidly swallowed up in the expenditure incurred in dealing with the steadily expanding traffic, and such savings often take the shape of avoidance of increased expenditure which it would otherwise have been imperative to incur.

In this way we can from the North Eastern Railway published accounts and figures trace a very definite avoidance of increase in for instance the amount of locomotive power as shown by the number of engines employed on that railway; that item is of course one of the most costly that appears in the accounts of a railway company. We may consider the figures shown in the following table :—

North Eastern Railway.

Year.	Tons of Freight Traffic Conveyed.	Engine Miles in Hauling Goods Train.	No. of Engines Available for Traffic.	Average Freight Train Load.
1882	38,741,635	14,283,834	1,462	—
1892	36,396,523	14,098,342	1,560	—
1894	44,351,405	15,642,906	1,830	—
1896	46,011,645	15,640,606	1,898	—
1898	50,403,657	16,800,086	1,994	—
1900	53,126,913	17,588,765	2,121	—
1902	50,383,778	14,932,815	2,142	81·40
1904	52,370,112	12,215,620	2,142	100·22
1906	56,348,255	12,338,303	2,000	109·92
1908	57,430,225	11,861,217	2,000	115·66
1910	58,785,814	11,326,338	2,000	126·52
1912	58,498,859	11,074,728	2,000	133·84
*	*	*	*	*
1919	49,670,969 Tons originating	12,240,536	2,000 12[1]	154·81

The principal facts which are apparent, and which may now be set out on perusing this table, are :—

(1) During the last twenty years of last century the growth of train mileage appeared to keep pace with the growth of traffic, and the increase of trains which this mileage represents necessitated a steady increase in the number of engines required to be used. This increase was at the rate of 6·6 per cent. in the ten years from 1882 to 1892, and 22·1 per cent. in the ten years from 1892 to 1902, or an increase of about 45 per cent. in the 20 years. The increase of tonnage carried was at the same time 30·05 per cent.

(2) The steady increase of train mileage and engines was arrested in the year 1902, and has been steadily declining ever since up to the outbreak of war.

(3) In 1902 the North Eastern Railway began to compile and publish their improved statistics.

(4) The number of engines which had so increased in the period from 1880 up to 1900 was found more than sufficient for the requirements of the traffic, and was actually reduced by taking 142 engines out of stock.

[1] New electric engines.

About 1905 the stock was curtailed to 2,000, and has remained at that figure ever since (except for the recent addition of 12 electric locomotives), although at the same time traffic had, up to the date of the war, been steadily growing.

(5) During the war it is generally understood that the train loading statistics were discontinued, and now that we again have figures to compare, the train mile figures begin to again show an increase, notwithstanding an apparently considerable drop in the number of tons conveyed.

I have referred to America as a country in which pre-eminently there has been a great development in the size of the freight train load. In that country the published figure of their freight train load is recorded in the annual reports of the Inter-State Commerce since 1888, and the average load of all the railway goods trains in America is as follows :—

Year.	Average Freight Train Load. Tons.	Year.	Average Freight Train Load. Tons.	Year.	Average Freight Train Load. Tons.
1888	176	1899	243	1910	380
1889	179	1900	270	1911	383
1890	175	1901	281	1912	430
1891	181	1902	296	1913	445
1892	181	1903	310	1914	452
1893	183	1904	307	1915	472
1894	179	1905	322	1916	550
1895	189	1906	344	1917	597
1896	198	1907	357	1918	628
1897	204	1908	352	1919	631
1898	226	1909	363	1920	647

This record tells a remarkable story : it tells on the face of it what has been happening—a persistent determination on the part of the American managers to improve and economise, showing that in less than thirty years they have more than three-folded the size of their train loads as the average figures in these records show.

Let us, however, beware lest we over-estimate the

importance of the factor of the big train load. It is important, but we must not make a fetish of it. As the train load increases, so in regular order must also the many appurtenances of railway equipment be enlarged, and these all tend to increase the cost of working.

Some of the many factors affecting the size of a train load, of which all need due consideration before any judgment as to the wisdom of any alteration of traditional methods of working can be pronounced, are set out below:—

(*a*) Variation in the nature of the traffic dealt with which may affect the figures.

(*b*) Number of stations and sidings per route mile which have to be catered for.

(*c*) The ratio of "pick-up" services to through train working.

(*d*) Gradients of the line.

(*e*) Capacity of locomotive stock.

(*f*) Facilities for dealing with traffic in the way of terminal exchange and marshalling yard accommodation and refuge sidings.

(*g*) Unremunerative branches, where for the convenience of the public a freight service of some sort *must* be given.

(*h*) Strength of bridges and viaducts.

The list of matters needing consideration in determining the size of a freight train that is practicable is sufficient to show the complexity of the problem: the study of these figures of load will serve to direct attention to most of these factors.

Almost equally surprising in America are the facts as to the rates charged for conveyance of freight traffic, and we give figures also under this head, as they afford a good illustration of how the record of average figures some years ago brought to the mind of railway managers and railway users (i.e. the traders) the fact that the steadily reducing freight charge had gone too far, and needed arresting. Let us present these figures: they are for the Pennsylvania Railroad, which may be taken as typical of U.S.A. as a whole:—

Freight Receipts per Ton per Mile on Railways in U.S.A. from 1870 to 1920.

Pennsylvania R.R. taken as a Sample.

Year.	Receipt per Ton per Mile. Cents.	Year.	Receipt per Ton per Mile. Cents.	Year.	Receipt per Ton per Mile. Cents.
1870	1·503	1888	0·693	1906	0·595
1871	1·354	1889	0·686	1907	0·577
1872	1·460	1890	0·655	1908	0·569
1873	1·443	1891	0·659	1909	0·580
1874	1·290	1892	0·626	1910	0·583
1875	1·126	1893	0·614	1911	0·587
1876	0·951	1894	0·585	1912	0·583
1877	1·014	1895	0·563	1913	0·583
1878	0·927	1896	0·564	1914	0·589
1879	1·824	1897	0·536	1915	0·610
1880	0·918	1898	0·499	1916	0·603
1881	0·857	1899	0·473	1917	0·631
1882	0·754	1900	0·540	1918	0·777
1883	0·881	1901	0·582	1919	0·879
1884	0·804	1902	0·586	1920	1·070
1885	0·695	1903	0·605		
1886	0·755	1904	0·605		
1887	0·730	1905	0·593		

From this table it is clear that at the same time that there has been a really great improvement and economy in working resulting from bigger train loads, the traders have also been to a large extent reaping, in the shape of reduced charges, the advantage of this economy. From 1870 to 1900 the table shows a steady reduction of rates, but with the turn of the century the railway managers, beginning to fear serious collapse if the process of reduction went on further, called a halt, and presenting the meaning of their figures to the public who use the railways, took steps to secure some increases in their charges ; so that since 1899, when the rates reached a nadir, the charges have been, generally speaking, again moving slightly upwards.

We have only been dealing in this chapter with what are known as "Operating Statistics," that is the figures which show the quantitative results of the internal railway working—the manipulation of traffic in wagons and trains. The subject is one capable of almost indefinite expansion, but we have singled out certain statistical units by way of illustrating some of the principal figures which have a direct bearing upon the principal factors in freight-train operating.

DAILY RETURN—GOODS TRAINS.

*Return for*____________________*191*____ *No.*____________ *Engine*______ *Class*________ *Driver*__________________ *Fireman*__________________

Departure from					Arrival at					MILES RUN EACH TRIP	NUMBER OF VEHICLES ATTACHED TO EACH TRAIN.									DETENTIONS.									Remarks as to Failure of Engine, Assistance given by another Company's Engine, &c.
STATION	Appointed Time		Actual Time.		STATION.	Appointed Time		Actual Time.			Goods.	Cattle	Fish	MINERAL.		Carriages.		Brake Vans.		AT	By Signals.		Waiting Load		Loco. Duties.		Other Causes.		
														Coal, Coke, Limestone, &c	Ironstone.	Loaded	Empty												
	H.	M.	H.	M.		H.	M.	H.	M.												H.	M.	H.	M.	H.	M.	H.	M.	

NOTE.—These columns do not include shunting.

Coal Received.		Water taken on Foreign Lines.		Shunting Trains at			Regular Pilot Work.				Interval of time away from the Engine, during the Shift, at		
STATION	Cwts.	STATION	Tanks	H	M		H.	M.	Shunting at	Disc. No.	H.	M.	

Hours of Duty.	A.M. OR P.M.	Driver.		Fireman.		Lodgings at	Driver or Fireman	s.	d.
		H.	M.	H.	M.				
Commenced Work at									
Left off Work at									
Hours on Duty	Total								
Do.	Weekday								
Do.	Sunday								

NOTE.—Work done for Permanent Way Department must in all cases be separately recorded and kept distinct from other work.

NOTE.—"Shunting" by TRAIN ENGINES includes only the time occupied by attaching, detaching, movements in yards or sidings, and interruptions between the commencement and finish of shunting with each train. Train shunting must in no case include detentions by signals before going into the yard, standing between the disposal of one train and the commencement of shunting another train, time occupied with loco. duties, or after shunting operations have entirely ceased.

NOTE.—In addition to Regular Shunting Engines, Pilot Work includes general shunting done by Train Engines, apart from dealing with their own trains.

Examined and Certified as Correct.

.................................Foreman.

.................................Station.

FIG. 6.—THE DRIVER'S REPORT (A.—— B.—— RAILWAY).

________ STEAM SHED.	ENGINE No.________	SHED LABEL ________
COMMENCED DUTY ON ________ (DATE) 19__ FINISHED DUTY ON ________ (DATE) 19__	CLASS ________	

	ON DUTY AT	*—RELIEVED *—LEFT ENGINE ON SHED AT	OFF DUTY AT	To be filled up by Office Staff. Total Time on duty. H.	M	Time for Payment. By Time.	By Mileage.
	(Station).	(Station).	(Station).				
DRIVER ________ No. ____	m.	m.	m.				
FIREMAN ________ No. ____	m.	m.	m.				
FIREMAN ________ No. ____	m.	m.	m.				

FULL DESCRIPTION OF TRAIN OR DUTY.	STATIONS STOPPED AT	ROUTE.	TRAIN TIME. Due from Starting Point H.	M.	Arrived. H.	M.	Departed. H.	M.	LOAD WHEN LEAVING EACH STATION. COACHING VEHICLES. Loaded.	Empty.	Coaching Tonnage.	FREIGHT WAGONS—excluding Working Brake Vans. Loaded. Goods.	Cattle.	Coal.	Other Minerals.	Empty. Goods.	Cattle.	Minerals.	Gross Tonnage including Working Brake Van.	SHUNTING. H.	M.	STANDING IN STEAM. H.	M.	LOCO. DUTIES. H.	M.	ASSISTANCE RENDERED. Train Engine.	Shed worked by	Req'd. or Not Req'd.
		*Whistled off or *Reman'd engine																										
		*Passed Disc. or *Engine reman'd.																										

This section to be filled up by Office Staff.

Service.	MILEAGE. Coaching.	Goods.
Train Miles.		
Regular Loaded		
" " Postal, Fish, etc		
" Empty		
" Engine and Brake ...		
Special Loaded		
" " *Postal, Fish, etc*		
" *Empty*		
" *Engine and Brake* ...		
Shunting Miles.		
Shunting Engines		
Train Engines		
Other Miles.		
Banking		
Required Assistant Engines ...		
Not Required Assistance ...		
Light Engine for traffic purposes		
Departmental, etc. Miles ...		
Total Engine Miles ...		
Grand Total Engine Miles		

ENGINE HOURS.	Coaching. H.	M.	Goods. H.	M.
Train Working (including Standing in Steam)				
Shunting—Shunting Engines				
" Train Engines				
Banking & Asst. Engines—(Required and Not Required)				
Light Engine—For Traffic Purposes				
Departmental, etc. Services				
Loco. Purposes: preparing and disposing of engine, etc. — Train Engines				
Shunting Engs				
Other Traffic Engs.				
Departmental etc., Engs.				
Total Engine Hours ...				
Standing in Steam by TRAIN Engines				

*—Strike out words not required

RELIEVED MEN BELONGING TO.................... (Station) .... RELIEVED BY MEN BELONGING TO.................... (Station).

Fig. 7.—The Driver's Report (C.—— D.—— Railway).

(Front of Form.)

NOTES FOR DRIVER.

1. Drivers should be very careful to give the **CORRECT** Engine Number and Shed Label Number.
2. A separate ticket must be used for each different Engine worked.
3. This ticket should be made out and left at the Time Office on completion of each turn of duty when booking off.
4. Drivers should, without fail, give in the "description of train or duty" column the **EXACT NATURE** of the train worked or other services performed, e. g., "Regular Empty Wagons," "**ASSISTING** Regular Passenger," "Light Engine," etc.

   N.B.—A train of Empty Wagons on which one or more loaded Goods Wagons are attached at any point, should be described as "Loaded Goods" throughout the trip.
5. The **TIME** actually occupied with loco. duties should be recorded in the column provided for the purpose. "Loco. Duties" are as follow, viz., preparing and disposing of engine, TAKING coal, examining engine, cleaning fires, engine repairs, etc.
6. Where there are alternative routes by which a train may travel, the one traversed should be shown, without fail.
7. Services of a departmental nature should be clearly described.
8. When men travel as Passengers the particular train by which they travel should be indicated in the "Train Time (due from starting point)" column.
9. One blank line must be left between the record of each separate train run or service.
10. The sections shewn below to be filled up when necessary.
11. The Shunter's signature is to be obtained for all regular or special passenger or goods shunting engine shunting.

STATE OF WEATHER.

REGULAR TRAINS DIAGRAMMED TO BE WORKED BY ENGINE, BUT DISCONTINUED.			
Description of Train.	Startin Time.	From	To

REGULAR TRAINS WORKED BY ENGINE, BUT DIAGRAMMED TO BE WORKED BY ANOTHER STATION.				
Station diagrammed to work Train.	Description of Train.	Starting Time.	From	To

DELAYS TO TRAINS INCLUDING LATE STARTS.			
Train.	Minutes	Station or other point where delay occurred.	Cause.

REMARKS.

Requisition No.............................received from.............................. *(Steam Shed Driver belongs to)*

Driver of Engine No..............................

Requisition No.............................handed to.............................. *(Steam Shed Driver belongs to)*

Driver of Engine No..............................

COAL LEFT ON TENDER AFTER FINISHING LAST TRIP FOR THE MONTH.

..............................CWTS.

ASSISTANCE RECEIVED.				
Assisting Engine. No.	Assisting Engine. Shed.	From	To	Cause of Assistance being required.

REGULAR AND SPECIAL SHUNTING.							
Description of Shunting.	Time Commenced Shunting. H.	Time Commenced Shunting. M.	Time Finished Shunting. H.	Time Finished Shunting. M.	Total Time Occupied. H.	Total Time Occupied. M.	Shunter's Signature.

SERVICES, ETC., RECEIVED ON FOREIGN RAILWAYS, SUCH AS COAL, OIL, WATER, PILOTS, ENGINES TURNED, FIRING UP, STABLING, ETC., ETC.		
Railway.	Station	Particulars of Service, giving weight or quantity of Coal, Oil, and Water.

FIG. 7.—THE DRIVER'S REPORT (C.—— D.—— RAILWAY).

(Back of Form.)

INDEX